JESUS
THE MESSIAH, THE SON OF GOD

AN EXPOSITION OF THE GOSPEL OF MARK FOR MEN

Spiritual Growth for Men

G. BRIAN CHRISTIE

ISBN 979-8-89130-159-7 (paperback)
ISBN 979-8-89130-160-3 (digital)

Christian Faith Publishing
832 Park Avenue
Meadville, PA 16335
www.christianfaithpublishing.com

Printed in the United States of America

CONTENTS

Preface...v

Chapter 1: Introduction to the Gospel of Mark 1
Chapter 2: The Early Miracles of Jesus............................ 5
Chapter 3: Jesus Calls His Disciples "Come, Follow Me" 9
Chapter 4: Jewish Rejection 14
Chapter 5: Jesus Turns to His Disciples........................... 20
Chapter 6: More Miracles for His Disciples 25
Chapter 7: You are the Messiah...................................... 30
Chapter 8: The Messiah Must Die 35
Chapter 9: Listen to Him.. 41
Chapter 10: Jesus Teaching on Marriage 45
Chapter 11: Be a Servant 50
Chapter 12: The Price for Our Freedom 54
Chapter 13: The Non-Triumphal Entry............................ 58
Chapter 14: Condemnation of the Temple........................ 62
Chapter 15: Give to Caesar What Belongs to Caesar
and to God What Belongs to God................. 66
Chapter 16: Total Commitment to God 70
Chapter 17: Be Faithful and Steadfast in the Midst
of Calamity 74
Chapter 18: The Resurrection Changes Everything............ 78
Chapter 19: The Lord's Supper 82

Chapter 20: Peter's Failures and Restoration........................ 86
Chapter 21: Religious Trial Before the Sanhedrin................ 90
Chapter 22: The Crucifixion of Jesus.................................... 95
Chapter 23: The Resurrection of Jesus 99

The purpose of this book

T his book is an exposition of the Gospel of Mark and is intended for Christian men who want to grow in their faith. We envision that our readers will be business-men who desire to follow Christ more earnestly and who want to live out their faith more consistently in their marriages, families, churches, neighborhoods, and especially in their careers. Our readers will range from those who have been in the faith for many years to those who are new in Christ. Most, but not all, will have college degrees, but all will be trying to live out their faith in their business arenas. Some will be lawyers and doctors, some will be real estate developers and home builders, some will be computer programmers and high-tech innovators, some will be in sales and marketing, and some will be electricians and plumbers. But all will have a desire to grow spiritually in their Christian faith.

The author

Your author is a businessman who has practiced law and been involved in various businesses over the past forty-five years. He is not a seminary professor or pastor or full-time Christian worker telling you how to live in a world he has not really experienced. So my perspective is that of a fellow traveler who has spent a lifetime immersed in the hurly-burly of the business world.

However, in addition to his law degree (JD, University of Texas), your author has a seminary degree (ThM, Dallas Theological Seminary, majoring in New Testament Greek). So this study will be soundly exegetical and theologically solid and, we trust, inspired by the Holy Spirit.

The context

This study was originally sent out in 2017 in twenty-five weekly emails to the men of Grace Fellowship Church in Costa Mesa, California, and about two hundred fifty other men from my various men's ministries over the years. I have not done much editing. I wanted to keep the style, circumstances, and energy of those emails written while I was daily deeply committed to my business—as a transactional ("deal") lawyer, business executive, director of two companies (one public), and an investor. Since I was born and raised in South Africa, you will see some occasional South African/British expressions and sentence structure. I have also not updated the time references for fear of losing the power and relevancy of each email at the time. So for instance, "last year" will mean 2016 and not 2022.

Each chapter can be read in about ten minutes designed for busy men. They can be read once a day for twenty-five days or as part of a men's Bible study group—a chapter or two a week. Or they can be read all in one go like a regular book. Since I am anticipating that most men will read one chapter a day or one a week in a men's Bible study group, there is significant repetition so that you don't have to keep flipping back to previous chapters to grasp the context. Also, repetition is, of course, a key to learning.

The purpose of those earlier emails—and this little book—is to encourage and strengthen Christian men in their walk with the Lord. Hopefully, the Holy Spirit will take the words of this book and use them to produce spiritual growth in all you men who take the time to read them.

My teachers

I came to faith in Christ as a teenager in Durban, South Africa. I was introduced to the Gospels by my first pastor, Pastor McPherson, at Bulwer Road Baptist Church in Durban. At Prairie Bible Institute, I was taught Mark by Mr. Maxwell and at Dallas Theological Seminary, and I was taught the Gospels by Dr. Dwight Pentecost.

In my library, I have two commentaries on the Gospel of Mark: *The Gospel of Mark by William Lane* (part of the *New International Commentary of the New Testament* series) and *Mark by R Kent Hughes* (part of the *Preaching the Word* series). I have taught the Gospel of Mark many times over the past forty-five years and have also heard it taught many times.

While I did not consciously rely on any outside commentary or reference work, I am sure that much of what I have written originally came from one of the sources mentioned in the previous paragraphs. When I do quote or consciously refer to a source, I try to attribute it to the immediate context.

My process

I have tried to write these chapters based on my own study of the Gospel of Mark. I use the study method I first learned from Prof. Howard Hendricks at Dallas Theological Seminary. I diagram each text in English (using the New International Version) and then do my own "observation, interpretation, application" process. Where appropriate, I will consult the underlying Greek text using *The Greek New Testament* edited by Aland et. al., Fifth Revised Edition.

My goal

As I wrote these chapters, I always had my readers in mind. Busy businessmen who wanted/needed spiritual strengthening and encouragement to face the challenges of that day. So while the exposition of each text is central, the end goal was always the relevant application of the text to the challenges and circumstances men face in their homes, businesses, neighborhoods, and sports. I constantly asked the Holy Spirit to lead and guide me as I wrote, and I am trusting that he will "strengthen you with power in your inner man" (Ephesians 3:16) as you read this book.

INTRODUCTION TO THE GOSPEL OF MARK

The beginning of the good news about
Jesus the Messiah, the Son of God.

—Mark 1:1

Background

The Gospel of Mark was most likely the first Gospel written. Early church history seems to confirm that the source of Mark's account of the life of Christ is Peter, who was both an eyewitness and an apostle. It was written in about AD 64 to the Christians in Rome who were undergoing persecution (probably from Nero). The language used indicates that the recipients were mostly Gentile Christians.

Good news

Some commentators think that "Christ the Servant" is the unifying theme of the Gospel of Mark. And they may be right, but while serving is emphasized at the end of chapter 10, it does not seem to be the main thrust of Mark. Rather, it seems to me that the very first verse of the Gospel of Mark (quoted above) sets out the purpose and main theme. The persecuted Christians in Rome needed to be encouraged by being reminded that the Jesus they had trusted was indeed the Messiah and the Son of God. So the purpose of Mark is to show that Jesus is the Messiah promised in the Old Testament, and equally important that He is the Son of God—truly divine.

Mark's approach

Mark writes in a no-frills, "just the facts" manner. He records eighteen fast-paced miracles that Jesus performed—casting out evil spirits, healings, raising the dead, walking on water, feeding the five thousand and the four thousand, calming the storm, and of course, the final and most significant miracle is His resurrection. These all showed that Jesus was indeed the Messiah and the Son of God.

And that's good news because if he is truly the Messiah and the Son of God, he has the power to forgive and provide eternal salvation to those who believe in him. No doubt, the devil had used the persecution to discourage them and tempt them to bail on their faith. Was all this suffering worth it?

So Mark sets forth a mostly chronological account of the life of Jesus. It begins with his forerunner, John the Baptist, and concludes with his resurrection and is highlighted by two confessions, the first by the apostle Peter and the second by a Roman centurion.

Peter's confession

Jesus initially preaches to the nation of Israel as a whole the "good news" that "the kingdom of God has come near; repent and believe the good news" (Mark 1:14–15). The reason it has "come near" is because Jesus the Messianic King has arrived. In spite of his many miracles, as the chapters unfold, we see the increased hostility of the leaders of the nation and their rejection of Jesus as the Messiah. So Jesus turns to his disciples and focuses on showing them that he is who he claims to be. The disciples and slow to respond, but finally in Caesarea Philippi, Peter, as the spokesman for the disciples, makes that great confession, "You are the Messiah" (Mark 8:29).

This is the tipping point in Jesus's ministry. The Jewish leaders (who represent the nation) have rejected him, but he now has the nucleus of disciples upon which the new form of the kingdom—the church—will be established. From this point on, his focus is on teaching and training the disciples in preparation for his departure. Then it is on to the cross, where he will bear the sin of the world and provide the foundation for good news.

The centurion's confession

After Jesus has been crucified by the Romans (at the instigation of the Jewish leaders), the Roman centurion, who was standing at the foot of the cross, watching and listening to Jesus's last words and actions, exclaimed, "Surely this man was the Son of God" (15:39). Mark intends this confession to be the climax to his Gospel. While most of the Roman soldiers had mocked and mistreated Jesus, here was one Roman soldier who witnessed the words and actions of Jesus on the cross and made this extraordinary confession. Whether he had previously heard Jesus teach or whether it was an insight given to him by the Holy Spirit, we don't know. But Mark's thrust is that not only Jesus's death but also his whole life, as recorded here by Mark, is evidence that Jesus really is the Son of God. He is God in the flesh!

The readers' confession

Clearly, Mark's purpose is that his readers (or hearers, since most could not read and would have this Gospel read to them, the persecuted believers in Rome) would come to the same conclusion after they read Mark's account of the life of Jesus. They had already believed in Jesus, been baptized, and were part of the church in Rome, but they needed encouragement. They needed to be powerfully and vividly reminded that Jesus really is the Messiah promised in the Old Testament, and that he really is the Son of God. His life, his words, and his miracles make that abundantly clear.

Our approach

We will work through some of the key sections in the Gospel of Mark in the following twenty-four chapters. In each chapter, I will quote some key verses discussed in that chapter. But time and space make it unwieldy to cite the larger section discussed in the chapter. For instance, in the next chapter, we look at the six miracles in chapters 1–3 of Mark's Gospel, but I only cite one of the miracles. So I encourage you to read the larger section (in this case chapters 1–3) of the Gospel as you read along.

I would also encourage you to read the entire Gospel of Mark in one go. It's the shortest Gospel. It's fast-moving. You can read it in under two hours. It is a vivid reminder that the Jesus we have trusted is really the Messiah and the Son of God. It will reenergize your faith.

CHAPTER 2

THE EARLY MIRACLES OF JESUS

Mark 1–3

When Jesus saw their faith, he said to the paralyzed man, "Son your sins are forgiven." Now the teachers of the law were sitting there thinking to themselves, "Why does this fellow talk like that? He's blaspheming! Who can forgive sins but God alone?" Jesus said to them, "Why are you thinking these things? Which is easier to say: to say to this paralyzed man, 'Your sins are forgiven' or to say, 'Get up, take your mat and walk.'" But I want you to know that the Son of Man has authority on earth to forgive sins. So he said to the man, "I tell you, get up, take your mat and go home." He got up and walked out in full view of them all. This amazed everyone and they praised God, saying, "We have never seen anything like this." (Mark 2:6–12)

Introduction

Mark's purpose is to encourage the Christians in Rome, who were undergoing persecution, by reminding them of who Jesus is—the Messiah and particularly the Son of God. And he does this in a fast-paced, vivid way.

The short introduction (Mark 1:1–13) begins with a brief account of the ministry of John the Baptist who prepared the way for Jesus by preaching a baptism of repentance to the nation of Israel in anticipation of the coming of the "one" who "will baptize you with the Holy Spirit." Then Jesus comes from Nazareth and is baptized by John in the Jordan River—accompanied by the voice from heaven announcing "You are my Son, whom I love; with you I am well pleased." The introduction concludes with Jesus's temptation in the wilderness.

Mark pretty much puts all his cards on the table in this introduction. He makes clear to the readers/hearers that the Jesus they have believed in is the Messiah, the Son of God. John the Baptist prepared his way—just as the Old Testament prophesied—and his public ministry was initiated by a voice from heaven, "You are my Son." The rest of the book substantiates these claims primarily through Jesus's actions and particularly his miracles.

Miracles, disciples, and hostility

In chapters 1–3, Jesus's early ministry in Galilee has three concurrent themes. The primary theme is the supernatural miracles of Jesus. The second is the calling of five of his disciples, which is important because a subtheme throughout the book is how Jesus nurtures his disciples through a growing understanding of who Jesus really is. And third, the growing hostility of the Pharisees and the Jewish leaders to Jesus's ministry—as early as chapter 3, they are plotting to kill him (3:6).

Jesus's miracles

There are six separate miracles in these first three chapters. First, Jesus goes to the synagogue in Capernaum to teach, and confronted with an impure spirit, he drives it out with authority (Mark 1:21–28). Second, he goes to Peter's house where he heals Peter's mother-in-law who was sick with a fever (Mark 1:29–31). Third, that evening He "healed many who had various diseases" and drove out more demons (Mark 1:32–34). These three miracle events in Capernaum (a town on the Sea of Galilee, which pretty much served as Jesus's headquarters in Galilee) demonstrated Jesus's power and authority. And the news of his miracles spread quickly. Moving away from Capernaum, Mark briefly records Jesus's fourth miracle when he heals a man with leprosy and sends him to Jerusalem to show his healing to a priest and follow the Old Testament ritual for cleansed lepers (Mark 1:40–45). Now Jerusalem was on notice that a miracle worker was present in Galilee.

Jesus's fifth miracle is the high point of these first three chapters, the healing/forgiving of the paralyzed man (Mark 2:1–12). And sixth, Jesus heals the man with the withered hand in the synagogue on the Sabbath, much to the annoyance of the synagogue leaders.

Healing of the paralyzed man (Mark 2:1–12)

Jesus is back in Capernaum, probably at Peter's house, preaching to an overflow crowd. Four men show up, carrying a paralyzed man for Jesus to heal. They can't get to Jesus because of the crowd. So they climbed onto the roof (as was customary, it was a flat roof) with the paralyzed man, made a hole in the roof, and lowered the mat with the paralyzed man on it, landing evidently right in front of Jesus as he was teaching. When Jesus saw their faith (the paralyzed man and his four friends), he says to the paralyzed man, "Son, your sins are forgiven." This gives the teachers of the law (Jewish teachers who had come to Capernaum to observe Jesus) heartburn! They know that only God can forgive sin and quickly put two and two together—this "man" is claiming to God! To them that was a clear case of blasphemy.

Jesus anticipated their thinking and promptly heals the paralyzed man demonstrating that he does indeed have the power to forgive. The man gets up takes his mat and walks out in front of all of them. The message is crystal clear; this Jesus is more than just a gifted rabbi or even a prophet. He is God! God has come to earth. It takes the rest of the book for the disciples to fully grasp this remarkable truth. And the Jewish leaders never get it, but it is true—Jesus is God!

Jesus is God

As Christians, we have staked our lives on this truth. Jesus is God the Son. He became incarnate (took on a human body and soul). Because he is God in the flesh, his death on the cross was sufficient to pay for the sins of the world. And because he is God, it is absolutely believable that he rose from the dead and ascended into heaven where he now sits at the right hand of the Father, soon to return as the glorious King and set up that promised future eternal kingdom. The message of Jesus is good news because it is true. He really is the Messiah, the Son of God. And we really will rule and reign with him eternally in the new heaven and earth. No matter how difficult the struggle in this life it is worth persevering.

CHAPTER 3

JESUS CALLS HIS DISCIPLES "COME, FOLLOW ME"

Mark 1–3

As Jesus walked beside the Sea of Galilee, he saw Simon and his brother Andrew casting a net into the lake, for they were fishermen. "Come, follow me," Jesus said, "and I will send you out to fish for people." At once they left their nets and followed him. When he had gone a little further, he saw James son of Zebedee and his brother John in a boat preparing their nets. Without delay he called them, and they left their father in the boat with the hired men and followed him. (Mark 1:16–20)

Context

In the introduction (Mark 1:1–13), Mark has disclosed to his readers/listeners that Jesus is the Messiah, the Son of God, that his ministry was initiated and authenticated by the voice from heaven declaring that "you are my Son," that he was led and assisted by the Holy Spirit, and would one day baptize believers with the Holy Spirit. The rest of the book demonstrates the truth of the introduction. Last week, we saw how his six early miracles in chapters 1–3 proved that he was not only the Son of God but also indeed God the Son.

The call of Simon, Andrew, James, and John

After the introduction, one of Jesus's first actions according to Mark is to call disciples to "follow me." Mark's account is so condensed that we want to try and flush out more details. Mark does not tell us why Jesus singled out Simon (Peter), Andrew, James, and John, nor why they surprisingly left their nets, business, and family to follow Jesus without taking time to think it over. We do not know whether they had previously heard Jesus preach about the coming kingdom of God (Mark 1:14–15), although they may have. The Gospels of John and Luke seem to make more sense to us in that they give some details about the events leading up to the disciples' decision to follow Jesus, and it is hard to avoid the temptation to import those few sketchy details into Mark's terse account.

The call of Levi

The call of Levi is similarly condensed:

> Once again Jesus went out beside the lake… As he walked along, He saw Levi the son of Alphaeus sitting at the tax collector's booth. "Follow me," Jesus told him, and Levi got up and followed him. (Mark 2:13–14)

This event takes place in Capernaum, which was a customs post on the trade route from Damascus to the Mediterranean Sea. Levi (whose surname is Matthew) was a Jewish tax official in the service of Herod Antipas, the ruler of Galilee. Such tax collectors were known for their corrupt practices and were generally despised by the Jews. Again, we see the same call and response—Jesus "told" him to "follow me," and he instantly leaves his post and follows Jesus. This is even more radical than the fishermen. They could go back to fishing, but once he had abandoned his toll collector's post, it was unlikely he could get his job back!

The call of the twelve disciples

The appointment of the twelve disciples in Mark 3:13–19 is similarly compressed:

> Jesus went up on a mountainside and called to him those he wanted, and they came to him. He appointed twelve that they might be with him.

Again, it seems so one-sided. Jesus is initiating all the action. Jesus is in control. The disciples seem to simply submit to his call. We don't know why Jesus chose these twelve. We would assume that they each had an individual call similar to the four fishermen and Levi.

It's all about Jesus

It seems to me that these calls to follow Jesus in Mark are intended to focus on Jesus's divine authoritative call and its immediate effects. Rabbis or teachers of the law in Jesus's day never called on people to "follow me." Instead, students sought out rabbis and teachers of the law who could teach them the Torah (the law), but the focus was on the Torah, not the teacher. These first disciples had not yet witnessed Jesus's miracle-working power and had no real idea of what following Jesus meant. They don't take time to mull over the call, and to be honest, they seem rather rash and impetuous!

The only explanation readers/hearers of Mark's Gospel (the Gentile Christians in Rome undergoing persecution and us today) can come up with for the sudden obedience of these disciples is that Jesus's call possesses divine power and in effect compels them to obey. Mark's point is that Jesus's divine and sovereign power alone, and not any human calculations or circumstances, causes them to obey and immediately follow him. Jesus calls, "Come, follow me," and it produces immediate submission and obedience from the disciples. It is an irresistible call.

He must be the Son of God

As the book unfolds, we hear Jesus's command the impure spirit, "Be quiet! Come out of him!" It submits and departs (Mark 1:25–26). Jesus commands, "Quiet! Be still!" The fierce wind stops, and the sea becomes "completely calm"

(Mark 4:39). Jesus commands, "Talitha koum! Little girl…get up!" and the dead child is raised from the dead (Mark 5:41–42). Jesus speaks, "Ephphatha! Be opened!" The deaf man's ears are opened (Mark 7:34–35). Jesus commands, "May no one ever eat fruit from you again," and a fig tree is withered from its roots (Mark 11:14, 20). Jesus utters a great cry from the cross, and the temple veil splits in two from top to bottom (Mark 15:38).

Takeaway

The sovereign and divine power of Jesus is the only explanation for why the disciples respond immediately to Jesus's call to "follow me." So the question Mark wants us readers to ask is not "Why did the disciples leave everything to follow him so abruptly?" but instead to ask, "Who is this who generates such immediate obedience?" He must be the Messiah. He must be the Son of God!

JEWISH REJECTION

Mark 1:14–15

> Jesus went into Galilee proclaiming the good news of God. "The time has come," he said, "the kingdom of God has come near. Repent and believe the good news." (Mark 1:14–15)

We are going to do some theology today. So put on your thinking cap! It's a little longer than usual, but it's key to understanding the gospels.

OT Background—the Davidic Covenant

In the Old Testament, God made four unconditional and eternal promises to the nation of Israel. These are the Abrahamic Covenant (Genesis 12), the Palestinian Covenant (Deuteronomy 30:1–10), the Davidic Covenant (2 Samuel 7), and the New Covenant (Jeremiah 31:33–37). The most prominent of these was the Davidic Covenant, which God made to

King David in about 1000 BC, in which God promised David that one of his descendants would be an eternal king who would set up an eternal earthly kingdom. This eternal and unconditional promise was originally made to David in 2 Samuel 7:12–16. The Psalms (e.g. Psalm 89 and 110), the prophets Isaiah (e.g. 9:6–7 and 11:4–5), Jeremiah (e.g. 33:15–17, 23:5–6 and 30:8–9), and Ezekiel and Hosea, Amos and Zachariah all constantly reaffirm this promise to the nation of Israel—that this descendant of David would be an eternal king who would set up an eternal earthly kingdom of peace, justice, and prosperity.

This promised king was referred to in Hebrew as the "Messiah" (which means "anointed one," because Israel's kings were anointed when they took the throne). "Christ" is the Greek translation of the Hebrew word *Messiah*. It is not Jesus's surname! It is a title. So Jesus Christ means Jesus the Messiah or Jesus the King.

The Davidic Kingdom

Ezekiel chapters 36–37 (about 600 BC, which is about four hundred years after David's death) clearly reiterates this promise of God and hope for the nation of Israel. Here's a small sample of this reiterated promise and hope for the nation of Israel:

> My servant David will be king over them, and they will have one shepherd. They will follow my laws and be careful to keep my decrees. They will live in the land I gave to my servant Jacob, the land where your ancestors lived. They and their children's children will live there forever, and David my servant will be their prince forever. I will make a covenant of peace with them; it will be an everlasting

> covenant. I will establish them and increase their numbers, and I will put my sanctuary among them forever. (Ezekiel 37:24–26)

It is clear that the Old Testament prophets expected a literal fulfillment of the Davidic Covenant through the promised Messiah. During the intertestamental period (from about 400 BC until the time of Christ when the nation of Israel was oppressed by the Greeks and then the Romans), the nation went through periods of time when their writings and actions showed that they were waiting expectantly for the Messiah, the "Son of David," to come and set up his promised earthly kingdom.

The kingdom of God has come near

So when Jesus came preaching the good news about the kingdom of God, the Jewish listeners knew exactly what he was referring to. He was referring to the promised earthly kingdom to be established by the promised descendant of David—a kingdom of peace, prosperity, and spiritual blessing under the Messiah's rule in the promised land, where the lion would lay down with the lamb, and swords and spears would be converted into plowshares.

It had "come near" because the Messiah Jesus had come to earth to set up this Messianic Davidic kingdom. This was indeed good news, but even though the promise was unconditional (in that God would fulfill it for certain), there was one condition to it being fulfilled "at that time." The nation of Israel needed to "repent and believe the good news."

The Davidic kingdom offered and rejected

We see in the first three chapters of Mark that Jesus clearly preaches that the nation of Israel must repent and accept him as the Messiah, the promised Son of David, who had come to set up the promised kingdom of God. But in spite of his miracles, his authoritative teaching, and his supernatural power, the leaders of the nation of Israel rejected him. As early as chapter 3, the Pharisees and Herodians were plotting to kill him (Mark 3:6), and the teachers of the law made that blasphemous response that Jesus was possessed by the devil (Mark 3:22). Mark's account sees this rejection in chapter 3 as a turning point. In chapter 4 onward, Jesus speaks to the people in parables only because of the hardness of their hearts.

The readers'/hearers' questions

The early Gentile Christians in Rome, whose only Bible was the Old Testament, needed answers to basic questions like these: (1) If Jesus is the Messiah promised in the Old Testament, why did Jesus not set up the promised eternal Davidic kingdom that Ezekiel promises? (2) What has happened to that eternal unconditional promise? (3) Why is the church full of Gentiles and so few Jews, and why is it suffering and persecuted? Is the church really God's kingdom on earth right now?

Jewish rejection of Jesus

A central theme in Mark is that the rejection of the offered Davidic kingdom by the Jewish leaders was not because there was some deficiency in Jesus. His whole Gospel is a demonstration that Jesus is the promised Messiah, the Son of God. But he does address these concerns. Jesus the Messiah did offer the promised Davidic kingdom to the nation of Israel (in chapters 1–3), but the nation would not repent and believe. In chapter 3, their hardness of heart and rejection becomes clear; thereafter, Jesus speaks to the people in parables and focuses instead on demonstrating to his disciples that he was indeed the Messiah, which they finally confess in chapter 8.

The kingdom parables

In chapter 4, Jesus tells various "kingdom parables," which he later explains to his disciples. Essentially the message of the kingdom parables is that in light of the Jewish rejection of Jesus and his Davidic kingdom, the kingdom of God would take a new "secret" interim form. The word *secret*, sometimes translated as "mystery," comes from the original Greek word *mysterion*, which theologically means something that was not revealed in the Old Testament but is now revealed in the New Testament. The present "secret" or "mystery" kingdom of God is the church, a spiritual kingdom, made up of Jews and Gentiles. Unlike the Davidic kingdom of immediate peace, justice, and prosperity for the nation of Israel, it will be international, start small and grow slowly, and suffer much persecution (see chapter 13).

This does not mean that God was "surprised" by Israel's rejection of Jesus. In his sovereignty, he preordained (or at least his sovereign plan allowed for) this rejection of a bona fide offer of the Davidic kingdom to Israel. This is why God's sovereign plan included the cross and the church. It's similar to God's repeated demand to Pharaoh to let Israel leave Egypt even though he knew (or preordained) that he would harden his heart and refuse.

The Davidic kingdom postponed

Since the promised earthly Davidic kingdom is an eternal covenant made to the nation of Israel, it cannot go unfulfilled. God's promises are always fulfilled. It must, therefore, be fulfilled in the future when the Messiah returns and the nation of Israel repents and believes in the Messiah. It is not ignored, withdrawn, or invalidated by the nation of Israel's rejection. Rather it is postponed for future fulfillment.

The new "secret" form of the kingdom of God

In the meanwhile (until Christ returns and the nation of Israel repents and accepts him as their promised Messiah), the church comprised of mostly Gentiles is the spiritual kingdom of God. It will start small, it will be persecuted and suffer, but it will slowly grow (as we will see in chapter 4). Following Christ in this interim period will be difficult and costly. It is not the promised Davidic kingdom. But in light of the rejection of Jesus the Messiah by the nation of Israel, the church is God's kingdom program until he returns to set up the earthly Davidic kingdom of God. We Gentiles enter this "kingdom" through faith in Jesus the Messiah

CHAPTER 5

JESUS TURNS TO HIS DISCIPLES

Mark 4:35–8:30

> He (Jesus) got up, rebuked the wind and said to the waves, "Quiet! Be still!" Then the wind died down and it was completely calm. He said to his disciples, "Why are you so afraid? Do you still have no faith?" They were terrified and asked each other, "Who is this? Even the wind and waves obey him!" (Mark 4:39–41)

The "unofficial" rejection of Jesus

In chapters 1–3, Mark portrays Jesus as proclaiming that the promised Davidic kingdom "had come near" because Jesus the Messiah, the Son of David, had come to earth. But in spite of his astounding miracles and authoritative teaching, the Jewish leaders refused the offer of the earthly Davidic kingdom.

In Mark's mind, the Jewish leaders "unofficially" rejected Jesus and his Davidic kingdom in chapter 3 when they began to plot to kill him and attributed his supernatural power to Satan. We say "unofficially" because the official rejection of Jesus the Messiah took place on Palm Sunday when he presented himself in Jerusalem on the prophetic day (Daniel 9) in the prophetic way (riding on a donkey, Zachariah 9:9) and with the prophetic announcement ("Hosanna to the Son of David"). But to Mark, the dye was cast by the end of chapter 3.

The "secret" form of the kingdom of God

Then in chapter 4, Jesus gives the "kingdom of God" parables. He essentially stops communicating clearly to the Jewish leaders and turns to his disciples. He tells them: "The secret of the kingdom of God has been given to you. But to those on the outside everything is said in parables" (Mark 4:11). The word *secret* translates to the Greek word *mysterion*, which means something not revealed in the Old Testament but is now revealed for the first time by Jesus. The rejection of the Messiah by the nation of Israel and the resulting failure to set up the promised earthly Davidic kingdom of peace, justice, prosperity, and spiritual blessing was not revealed in the Old Testament. But now that they were rejecting him, the kingdom of God would take a new "secret" form (which of course was preordained by God in his sovereignty). Only a minority would accept the Word (parable of the Sower and the seed), and it would start small but slowly grow (parable of the mustard seed), but God, in his sovereignty, will ensure that it grows and matures until the final judgment (parable of the seed growing by itself). It would be a spiritual kingdom significantly different from the promised earthly Davidic kingdom (which will be postponed and only inaugurated when Jesus returns).

Jesus turns to his disciples

Beginning in 4:35 and concluding in 8:29, where the disciples finally confess, "You are the Messiah," Jesus focuses primarily on demonstrating to the disciples that he is the Messiah, the Son of God.

In the first half of this section, Jesus performs four amazing miracles exclusively or primarily for the benefit of the disciples—the calming of the storm, the restoration of the man possessed by a legion of demons, the healing of the woman who touches him, and the raising of Jairus's daughter from the dead. These miracles demonstrate to his disciples that Jesus is the Messiah, the Son of God. We will look at the first one, which takes place immediately after the giving of the "secret" kingdom of God parables.

The calming of the storm

This miracle is performed exclusively for the disciples. No one else is present. Jesus instructs his disciples to get into the boat and go over to the other side of the Sea of Galilee. While they were following his direction, a "furious squall" came up and nearly swamped the boat. Jesus was in the stern of the boat, sleeping! The disciples wake him, exclaiming, "Don't you care if we drown?" There are two complaints here. "First, we were following your instructions to get into the boat and set out for the other side—so it's your fault that we are in this deadly storm! And second, why are you sleeping when we are about to drown following your directions?"

Jesus has power over nature

In response to their complaint, Jesus "rebukes" the wind and waves, and immediately the wind dies down, and the sea becomes completely calm. And then he says to the disciples, "Why are you afraid? Do you still have no faith?" This was the first of many tests where Jesus is looking for the disciples to respond by believing that he is the Messiah and that he will protect them in the storm, but they failed the test. They freaked instead of exercising faith!

But in spite of their lack of faith, Jesus miraculously calmed the storm. Jesus is demonstrating to his disciples that he has power over the forces of nature. The winds and the waves obey him!

Takeaway

The disciple's response, "Who is this? Even the wind and the waves obey him!" It is Mark's major point in recounting this miracle. He is saying to his readers/listeners (and to us): This Jesus you have believed in is the supernatural Messiah. In the midst of persecution and difficulties, don't doubt the truth of the gospel. Jesus is truly the Messiah. He is God in the flesh. The gospel is built on this foundational truth.

But a second point emerges. Sometimes it appears that when we are trying to follow Christ and his instructions, we end up in a storm! He cares and can calm the storm at any time. In the storm, he wants us to trust him with the outcome. Like the disciples, he uses the storms to develop our faith. The disciples failed this test, but in his grace, Jesus calmed the storm anyway and prepared them for the next test. Trust him in the storms of your life. He is truly the Messiah, God the Son!

An interesting thought: Weak faith sometimes results in Jesus miraculously dismissing our "storm," whereas mature strong faith often involves going through the "storm" with Jesus with the resulting spiritual growth, strengthened faith, and maturity.

CHAPTER 6

MORE MIRACLES FOR HIS DISCIPLES

Mark 6–7

*C*ontext Mark 6–7. Having been "unofficially" rejected by the Jewish leaders in chapter 3 and after giving the kingdom of God parables to the people (and later explaining them to the disciples), Jesus turns his primary attention in chapters 5–8, convincing his disciples that he is the Messiah. In this chapter, we will look at chapters 6–8, where Mark's major point is that Jesus's miracles are intended to demonstrate to the disciples that Jesus really is Messiah and particularly to trust Him. But these chapters also chronicle the increasing hostility and rejection of Jesus by the Jewish people and particularly their leaders.

Rejection, suffering, and conflict

Chapter 6 begins with Jesus returning to his hometown of Nazareth, where he is rejected and mocked. Then also in chapter 6, Mark gives a long-detailed account of the beheading of John the Baptist, the Messiah's forerunner, by King Herod. In chapter 7, we find some Pharisees and the teachers of the law who had come to Galilee from Jerusalem, challenging Jesus regarding his disciples not washing their hands before eating. This led to a real confrontation where Jesus exposes their hypocrisy and how they used religious "dodges" to circumvent their genuine obligation to support their parents. Clearly, opposition and hostility toward Jesus are building significantly.

Miracles

There are four amazing miracles in these two chapters performed primarily for the benefit of bringing the disciples to the conviction that Jesus is the Messiah. Jesus fed the five thousand, he walked on water, he heals the Gentile woman's daughter, and he heals the deaf and mute man.

There is actually a fifth miracle where Jesus sends out the twelve disciples and gives them miraculous authority to cast out demons and heal the sick, which they did successfully. His unique instruction to the twelve was that they were to "take nothing for the journey except a staff—no bread, no bag, and no money in your belts." This is a key point: He wanted them to trust him, the Messiah, to provide for their needs. And he did!

Feeding of the five thousand

This is the only miracle (other than the resurrection) mentioned in all four Gospels. So the Gospel writers (and God the real author) think this is an important miracle! We all know the story. The disciples were baffled as to how they could provide food for all these people in a deserted place. Their answer was to send them away to try and find somewhere to buy food (good luck!).

The heart of the miracle and message is that Jesus takes the very little food they could come up with—five loaves and two fish—and miraculously provides a satisfying meal for over five thousand people!

This reinforces Jesus's message to the disciples when they went on their mission with no supplies: "Trust me, I will provide. I can take your small resources and multiply them to meet your needs. I can do this because I am the Messiah. I am the Son of God. Trust me!"

Not only did Jesus provide the meal, but twelve basketfuls of overflow were collected by the disciples. Perhaps this is an allusion to Moses through whom God provided daily manna for the Israelites in the wilderness. But the significant difference is that the manna could not be kept overnight—it went bad if kept overnight. But when Jesus provides, there is overflow—much leftover for the next day. The point is that Jesus is greater than Moses! Moses was a prophet and lawgiver. Jesus is the Messiah, the Son of God!

Rejection and persecution are expected

The Gentile Christians in Rome—who were the original recipients of Mark's Gospel—were undergoing significant rejection and persecution for their faith. They could identify with Jesus and his rejection by his hometown and family, with John the Baptist's death at the hands of a cruel king, and with the disrespectful treatment of Jesus by the religious leaders. Mark's message to them is that their suffering is not because they were on the wrong path or because they were sinning in some perfectionistic way. Rather, their rejection and persecution were just like their Savior's. They were walking in his footsteps. There is no prosperity gospel. This is not heaven, this is not the Davidic kingdom, and this is not the new heaven and earth. Rejection and persecution are the norm for faithful believers.

Here in the United States, we have been spoiled because for so long, it has been relatively easy to be a Christian, and our values have, in fact, often been lauded. Faithful believers have often prospered. But our culture is turning, and now many of our values and convictions (e.g., a marriage is between one man and one woman, our pro-life stance, only one way to God, and that is through faith in Christ, and so on) are considered radical and even bigoted and hateful! Some Christian businesses and businessmen who have taken a stand on these issues are being boycotted or sued. We may be entering a period where our faith in Christ will be costly, and we, too, will be marginalized. Jesus said these sobering words, "If the world hates you, keep in mind that it hated me first… A servant is not greater than his master. If they persecuted me, they will persecute you also" (John 15:18–20). If such rejection and suffering do come our way, we will be walking in the steps of our Messiah.

Trust him to provide

The Christians in Rome were particularly suffering financially. They were kicked out of the trade guilds. People boycotted their businesses. They were being squeezed financially. So the account of Jesus taking the "little" (five loaves and two fishes) and miraculously providing for the needs of five thousand would have been so encouraging. This is one of Mark's emphases. Jesus is the Messiah. He provided for the needs of his disciples on their missionary journey and for the five thousand by the lake. He can and will provide for your needs. Trust him!

Are you going through a difficult patch? Where your resources seem so little? God may be reaching out to you and saying, "Trust me. I am the Messiah. I fed the five thousand. I will provide for you." Trust him!

CHAPTER 7

YOU ARE THE MESSIAH

Mark 8:1–30

Aware of their discussion, Jesus asked them: "Why are you talking about having no bread? Do you still not see or understand? Are your hearts hardened? Do you have eyes but fail to see, and ears but fail to hear? And don't you remember? When I broke the five loaves for the five thousand, how many basketfuls of pieces did you pick up? "Twelve," they replied. And when I broke the seven loaves for the four thousand, how many basketfuls of pieces did you pick up? They answered, "Seven." He said to them, "Do you still not understand?" (Mark 8:17–21)

Context

Since the unofficial rejection of Jesus by the Jewish leaders (chapter 3), Jesus's ministry has focused primarily on demonstrating to his disciples that he is the Messiah. He has performed at least eight separate identifiable miracles: calming the storm, restoring a demon-possessed man, healing the bleeding woman, raising a dead girl, feeding the five thousand, walking on water, driving out the demon from the Gentile woman's daughter, and healing the deaf and mute man. He also performed Mass healings, including healing those who touched his cloak and gave the disciples the power to heal and cast out demons on their missionary journey. But all throughout this period, the disciples are slow to understand. For instance, after witnessing Jesus feed the five thousand and then walking on the lake, Mark records: "They were completely amazed, for they did not understand the loaves; their hearts were hardened" (6:52).

Jesus feeds the four thousand (8:1–10)

Another large crowd had been with Jesus for three days. Jesus has compassion for them and shares with his disciples his desire that they be fed. Jesus is clearly looking for the disciples to respond in faith (after just recently witnessing the miraculous feeding of the five thousand, not to mention all the other miracles) and say something like this, "You are the Messiah. Here is the small amount of food we can gather, but we give it to you, trusting you to miraculously multiply it to feed this multitude. We trust you!"

But instead, they respond, "But where in this remote place can anyone get enough bread to feed them?" You can almost hear Jesus's sigh of disappointment when he says, "How many loaves do you have?" and goes ahead and miraculously feeds the four thousand with seven loaves and a few fish.

The disciples don't get it (Mark 8:11–21)

Shortly after the feeding of the four thousand and a brief confrontation with the Pharisees, Jesus and his disciples are on a boat crossing the lake. The disciples misunderstand Jesus's warning about the corrupting influence of the legalistic and hypocritical teaching of the Pharisees. They think he is admonishing them for not bringing enough bread for the journey. This leads to the seven penetrating questions that Jesus asks his disciples that are quoted above. Essentially, he is saying, "Don't you understand who I am? Why are you worried about not having enough bread when you have seen me provide enough for nine thousand men to eat with basketfuls left over? You've seen all my miracles, you've heard my authoritative teaching, and you've been with me for over two years. Don't you yet understand that I am the Messiah?"

The disciples get it—at least somewhat! (Mark 8:22–30)

After another miracle (healing of the blind man in Bethsaida), Jesus took the disciples to the area of Caesarea Philippi (to the far north of Galilee), where Jesus brings it to a head. "Who do people say I am?" After initially evading the heart of the question by referring to what "others" believed (John the Baptist or Elijah), Jesus brings them to their "come to Jesus" moment, "But what about you? Who do you say I am?"

Peter, speaking for the disciples, makes the great confession, "You are the Messiah."

The disciples finally get it—at least that Jesus is the Messiah. As we will see in the next few weeks, they still had a lot to learn. But they had made the key decision; this "man" Jesus is the Messiah! Clearly, for Mark, this is the key turning point in his Gospel. Up until this point, the question Mark has been posing and answering has been: Who is this Jesus? From this point forward, the question he is answering is: What kind of Messiah is he, and what does it mean to follow this Messiah?

Jesus is the Messiah

Remember, the overall purpose of the Gospel of Mark was to demonstrate to the original readers/hearers that Jesus is the Messiah, the Son of God (Mark 1:1). They were mostly Gentile Christians in Rome who were being persecuted, ostracized, and marginalized for their faith. I'm sure the devil, not to mention their own sinful natures, periodically put doubts in their minds. Is Christianity really the true way? Is Jesus really the Messiah, the Son of God? Are we suffering for the true way to God? Or are we following a myth? Is our little house church really the presence of God in Rome?

They could identify with the disciples. The leadership and majority of the people in Rome had rejected Jesus, but they believed. Perhaps they had been just as spiritually obtuse as the disciples until God opened their eyes to the truth, and they, like Peter, confessed, "You are the Messiah."

But as they heard Mark's recounting the miracles of Jesus (some of which may have been new to them), they would have been encouraged and along with the disciples would have reaffirmed their faith in Jesus. Yes, he really is the Messiah. Yes, we are following the truth of God.

Takeaway

We, too, can identify with the disciples. Even though, like the disciples, I am often spiritually slow and obtuse. I really do believe that Jesus is the Messiah, the Son of God. I trust Him. I trust him with my eternal destiny. I trust him with my life. I trust him with my family. I trust him with my business. I trust him on the mountain. I trust him in the valley. I trust him for what lies ahead today.

THE MESSIAH MUST DIE

Mark 8:31–38

We have now reached a key section in Mark's Gospel (8:31–38). The verses below try to capture the essence of this section, but it would be beneficial to read all eight verses.

> He then began to teach them that the Son of Man must suffer many things and be rejected by the elders, chief priests and the teachers of the law, and that he must be killed and after three days rise again. (Mark 8:31)

> Whoever wants to be my disciple must deny themselves and take up their cross and follow me. (Mark 8:34)

> When he (the Son of Man) comes in his
> Father's glory with the holy angels. (Mark
> 8:38)

The context

The key words in this section are "He then began" in verse 31. It was only after the disciples had confessed that Jesus was the Messiah (Mark 8:29) that Jesus makes these three revelations to the disciples. Only now were they ready for this next step. Even so, they really did not understand the significance of these revelations. These revelations answer the two key questions that Mark addresses in this second half of his Gospel—what kind of Messiah is Jesus, and what does it mean to follow Jesus as his disciple?

The three great revelations

These are the key revelations (which will be developed as the chapters unfold): First, Jesus the Messiah will suffer, be rejected, and then be killed by the Jewish religious leaders, but after three days, he will rise again. Second, following Jesus involves self-denial, suffering, and sacrifice. Third, glory is not now, it lies in the future when Jesus returns.

Theological perspective

All three of these revelations were exactly the opposite of what the disciples were expecting. The Old Testament promised that when the Messiah came, he would establish for the nation of Israel an eternal kingdom of peace, prosperity, spiritual blessing, and God's glory here on earth. So once the disciples confessed that Jesus was the Messiah, they expected that he would go to Jerusalem and set up the promised Davidic kingdom and that they would be a significant part of this great kingdom. But what they did not understand is that although the promise of the glorious earthly Davidic kingdom is an unconditional and eternal promise, the timing of its fulfillment depended on the nation of Israel accepting Jesus as the Messiah. Instead, they were rejecting him and planned to kill him. So the fulfillment of the promise of the glorious Davidic kingdom will be postponed until the return of the Messiah to earth in the future.

The Messiah must die

This disclosure that Jesus must suffer, be rejected, and be killed by the Jewish religious leaders is repeated three times—here in 8:31, in 9:30–31, and again in 10:32–34. This is the central revelation. In 8:31–10:52, Mark records how the disciples respond to this prediction of his death and the lessons of discipleship that emerge from this interaction.

Peter, again speaking for the disciples, "rebukes" Jesus for this prediction of his death. Jesus responds by attributing his reaction to the influence of Satan. Peter could not comprehend how the Messiah, once known, could be rejected and killed by his chosen nation. It seemed to be so contrary to the kingdom's promises about the Messiah in the Old Testament.

Isaiah 53 and Psalm 22

Some theological perspective. The broadband of Messianic promises in the Old Testament are about the glorious earthy Davidic kingdom of peace, prosperity, and spiritual blessings for the nation of Israel. However, there is another much smaller band of prophecies regarding the suffering and death of the Messiah. Isaiah 52:13–53:12 prophesies about a "suffering servant," who would be "despised and rejected" (vs. 3), who would be "pierced because of our rebellion, crushed because of our iniquities, the punishment for our peace was on him, and we are healed by his wounds" (vs. 5). This suffering servant would be "punished by the Lord for the sin of us all" (vs. 6). He would be "led like a lamb to be slaughtered" (vs. 7), and the Lord would "crush him severely" and "make him a guilt offering" (vs. 10).

Psalm 22 is a Messianic psalm of David where David's suffering foreshadows the sufferings of the Messiah. As we will see when we get to the crucifixion, on the cross, Jesus cried out David's words in verse 1, "My God, my God, why have you forsaken me?"

The animal sacrifices

The whole Jewish worship system revolved around animal sacrifices, the burnt offering (which was offered every morning and evening in the temple), the sin offering, the guilt offering (referenced in Isaiah 53:10 above), and the fellowship offering. The major annual festivals like Passover and the Day of Atonement centered on the animal (a lamb, goat, or bull) that had to die in the place of the worshippers. By the laying on of hands, the sin of the offerors was metaphorically transferred to the unblemished animal, which was then killed for the sins of the offerors as their "substitute." So the concept of a "substitute" animal that needed to die in the place of the sinners was a requirement for the worshippers to be forgiven and accepted by God. It was obvious that the death of animals could not wipe away human sin. The animal sacrifices foreshadowed the Messiah who would die once and for all for the sins of the world.

Two strands of prophecy

Jewish scholars struggled with these two strands of prophesy—a Messiah who would be an Eternal King, setting up an eternal kingdom, and on the other hand, a suffering servant who would be rejected, despised, crushed for our sin, and be killed as a guilt offering. One theory was that there would be two Messiahs—one to die and one to reign! In hindsight, we now know that there would be only one Messiah, Jesus, who would both die (at his first coming) and reign (at his second coming).

The point in this context is that Peter and the other disciples (for whom he was the spokesman) were focusing only on the reigning Messiah and his glorious earthly kingdom. But as Mark 1:14–15 made clear that the prerequisite for Jesus to inaugurate the glorious Davidic kingdom was for the nation of Israel to "repent and believe." But they did not repent and believe that Jesus was the Messiah. Instead, they rejected him and planned to kill him. God, in his sovereignty, knew this and had David and the prophets prophesy, this seemingly contradictory prophecy, that the Eternal King who would set up the eternal kingdom would be rejected, despised, and killed. No wonder Peter and the disciples were confused.

Jesus will rise again

Although all three predictions of his death conclude with the promise, "After three days, he will rise again," it seems that the disciples totally missed it. The resurrection is, of course, the key to understanding how the Messiah could die and yet one day fulfill the Old Testament promises of the earthly Davidic kingdom.

What it means to follow Jesus (Mark 8:34–38)

Self-denial and willingness to die for Jesus (taking up your cross) is the essence of discipleship and not being ashamed of Jesus in this fallen world. The original readers/hearers would have identified with these verses because persecution and ridicule could tempt them to deny their commitment to Jesus. For us, it is peer pressure and perhaps fear of ridicule that tempts us to be closet Christians. This theme of discipleship is central to the next two chapters.

Glory comes later

The disciples like us wanted glory now. In their case, they wanted the earthly Davidic kingdom of peace, prosperity, spiritual blessings, and God's manifest presence immediately after they confessed Jesus as the Messiah. For us, deep down inside, we really want heaven on earth now. Even though theologically we reject the prosperity gospel, our prayers and hopes are for our lives to be heaven on earth now—perfect families and children, continual business success, and freedom from failure, trials, and grief. But heaven and glory will only come in the future when Jesus "comes in his Father's glory with the holy angels." In the meanwhile, we are fallen people (although partially restored by the Holy Spirit) living in a fallen world surrounded by fallen people, and Satan goes around like a roaring lion seeking to devour us! Faithfulness and perseverance in this "non-heaven" world are our calling! Heaven and glory come later.

LISTEN TO HIM

Mark 9:1–10

The well-known account of Jesus's transfiguration in Mark 9:1–10 provides a key lesson in what it means to be a disciple of Jesus. Here are some select verses from that account:

> After six days Jesus took Peter, James, and John with him and led them up a high mountain where they were alone. There Jesus was transfigured before them. (Mark 9:2)

> And there appeared before them Elijah and Moses, who were talking with Jesus. (Mark 9:4)

> Then a cloud appeared and covered them, and a voice came from the cloud: 'This is my Son, whom I love. Listen to him. (Mark 9:7)

Confusion

The disciples, and especially Peter their spokesman, were totally confused. They had finally confessed that Jesus was the Messiah (Mark 8:29). They expected that this meant that Jesus the Messiah, the Son of David, would soon be moving toward Jerusalem to set up the glorious Davidic kingdom of peace, prosperity, and spiritual blessings in Israel as promised in the Old Testament. But instead, Jesus immediately revealed to them that he was going to be rejected and killed by the Jewish religious leadership. He also told them that following him as a disciple involved self-denial, sacrifice, suffering, and a willingness to lose oneself for Jesus and the gospel. And that there would be no "glory" now—it would be postponed until his second coming. Peter and the disciples were absolutely confused. This is not what they understood they were committing to when they confessed Jesus as the promised Old Testament Messiah, the Son of David. I'm sure they were thinking: Is this Jesus really the Messiah? Is he really from God? Are we following God's true Messiah?

Reassurance

The first purpose of the transfiguration seems to be reassurance—to reassure and reaffirm to the chosen disciples that Jesus really is the Messiah. And that they were following God's true way by committing their lives to follow him. The transfiguration also serves as a "sneak preview" of what glory will be like when Jesus returns to the earth "with his holy angels."

Jesus selects Peter, James, and John for this special experience. The mountain is probably Mount Hermon about twelve miles northeast of Caesarea Philippi where the disciples had made their great confession. Jesus is "transfigured" before them.

The Greek word used for "transfigured" is *metamorphothe* (from which we get the word metamorphosis). It means to change into another form, not just a change in outward appearance. For a brief time, Jesus's human body was transformed into the glorious body he will possess when he returns in glory to set up his glorious kingdom on earth. Moses (the lawgiver and liberator) and Elijah (the representative of the prophets) appeared with Jesus.

This is my Son

Peter wanted to build three shelters, one each for Moses, Elijah, and Jesus, perhaps unwittingly implying that he saw all three as equal. But immediately the voice from the cloud clarifies this: "This [that is, Jesus] is my Son whom I love." Moses and Elijah were great servants of God, but Jesus is the Messiah, the Son of God. This would have greatly reassured and encouraged the three disciples who witnessed Jesus's transfiguration and heard the heavenly voice. They may still not have understood the significance of the three confusing revelations Jesus had made to them six days earlier. But one thing they now knew for sure was that Jesus was indeed the Messiah, the Son of God!

Listen to him

Then the voice of God the Father from the cloud adds these keywords: "Listen to him." These words look both backward and forward. They, no doubt, are intended to look back to three great revelations Jesus had made to the disciples six days ago. Even though they flew in the face of the expectations of the disciples, the Father is reaffirming them as his will and way. And these words look forward to the lessons that Jesus is about the teach the disciples in the next two chapters regarding what it means to be a disciple of Jesus. But the overarching lesson to the three disciples on the mountain with Jesus—and the original readers of Mark's Gospel—is to "listen to him." Listening to Jesus is Job One for a disciple!

However, the word *listen* in the original Greek text has the idea of "hear and obey." We use it this way in English as well. Have you ever said to your kids in an emphatic voice: "Listen to me when I tell you to. We don't mean just hearing what I am saying. We mean "obey what I am telling you to do!" Jesus wants us not just to hear but far more importantly to obey. Obedience to Jesus is the real mark of a disciple.

Takeaway

The application is obvious. We want to follow Jesus, and we want to be his disciples. The first lesson in discipleship is "listen to him." How do we do this?

Jesus speaks to us primarily through the Word of God—the Bible. The mark of a disciple is that they are men of the Word. They "listen" to Jesus as he speaks through his Word. They have a regular discipline of reading and studying God's Word, both individually and in group Bible studies. Perhaps this is a time for a recommitment to a regular (daily?) time in God's Word. But hearing is not enough. Obeying what we read and hear is what God is looking for in a disciple.

CHAPTER 10

JESUS TEACHING ON MARRIAGE

Mark 10:1–12

In Mark chapters 9 and 10, Jesus is teaching his disciples what it means to be His disciple. By my count, there are ten lessons he teaches them. We looked last week at the key lesson learned from Jesus's transfiguration—listen to Jesus. Today we will look at how a follower of Jesus should view marriage as seen in Mark 10: 1–12. Here are the key verses:

> But in the beginning of creation God made them male and female. For this reason a man will leave his father and mother and be united to his wife, and the two will become one flesh. So they are no longer two but one flesh. Therefore, what God has joined together let no one separate. (Mark 10: 6–9)

Context

Jesus and his disciples are leaving Galilee and moving south toward Jerusalem where Jesus will be formally rejected and killed. This teaching takes place in Perea, just on the east side of the Jordan River. Some Pharisees tried to trap Jesus with this loaded question, "Is it lawful for a man to divorce his wife?" There were two schools of doctrine regarding marriage and divorce in Palestine at that time. Rabbi Hillel taught that a man could divorce his wife for pretty much any reason—as long as he gave her a certificate of divorce. But Rabbi Shammai taught that divorce should not be allowed except for serious moral failure. But the real trap was that King Herod had capriciously divorced his wife and married his brother's wife, which John the Baptist had publicly exposed and which ultimately cost him his head! The Pharisees want Jesus to step into this messy arena, hoping that Jesus would answer in a way that would offend Herod or one of the Jewish groups.

Moses

Jesus first asks them what Moses had to say about marriage and divorce. They replied with a twist on Deuteronomy 24:1–4, "Moses permitted a man to write a certificate of divorce and to send her away." Moses had permitted divorce if the husband gave the wife a certificate of divorce. The purpose of this instruction was not to sanction divorce but to protect the wife being divorced. The certificate of divorce gave proof that the wife was released from the marriage contract and affirmed her right to remarry. Jesus makes it clear that Moses only permitted divorce because "your hearts were hard" and that divorce had never been part of God's plan for his people.

Jesus

Jesus responds with his clear teaching on marriage and divorce set out in the verses I quoted above. He goes back to the creation account and makes at least four critical points: (1) God created mankind as males and females and that marriage is between a male and a female, (2) the man and the woman are to "leave" their parents (physically, emotionally, and financially) and be "united" to each other, (3) the married man and woman are "no longer two, but one flesh," and (4) marriage is intended to be a permanent union. Marriage is to be a monogamous, heterosexual, permanent, one-flesh relationship.

The word *man* in the command of Jesus, "What God has joined together, let no man separate," is the word that means "male." So it does not refer to the judicial authority granting the divorce but to the husband, commanding him to not violate the one-flesh relationship by initiating a divorce.

Remarriage

Mark's account of Jesus's teaching is very clear: "Anyone who divorces his wife and marries another woman commits adultery against her" (vs. 11) and vice-versa for the wife (vs. 12). God takes the permanence of the one-flesh marriage relationship seriously! Mark's account is no exception. However, Matthew's account does allow an exception for "marital unfaithfulness," which probably means persistent, unrepentant sexual unfaithfulness, not a one-time fall. God's desire for a broken marriage is forgiveness and reconciliation. Paul solemnly reinforces this requirement: "To the married I give this command (not I but the Lord): a wife must not separate from her husband. But if she does, she must remain unmarried, or else be reconciled to her husband. And a husband must not divorce his wife" (1 Corinthians 7:10–11).

Discipleship

Committed followers of Christ embrace Jesus's teaching on marriage and divorce. Back in the early eighties, I discipled a young man named John Wayland, and he and Debbie soon got married after his graduation from Southwestern University in Georgetown, Texas. More than twenty years later, John wrote these words in describing how a disciple of Jesus views and commits to his marriage (something he is now living out in his marriage to Debbie):

> A marriage is meant to be a place to live out unconditional love. It is a place to learn what it is to give rather than to take. It is designed to be a safe place to develop trust as we learn to develop vulnerability. It is where we learn what love can really be… "Two becoming one flesh" is not just a nice concept to be considered. It is not just something to say at weddings, while we wait for the cake to be cut. "Two becoming one flesh" is God's design for the people He desperately loves. Marriage is a living and breathing picture of how Christ and His church are intimately and permanently connected.

For those of you reading this who have fallen in this area, embrace God's grace and forgiveness. The past is over. It is forgiven. Move forward from where you are today.

Takeaway

For those of us in marriage (whether first or second or even third), we need to proactively commit to Jesus's teaching here on marriage and divorce. Marriage can really be the safe, intimate, and permanent relationship that John envisions. I can be great. A mark of a disciple of Jesus is that he is committed to living out the one-flesh relationship with his wife. After his relationship with God, it is his top priority—and how he spends his time and money reflects this.

BE A SERVANT

Mark 10:35–45

Muhammed Ali, the great heavyweight boxer, died recently. When he was in his prime, he used to frequently announce before or after a big fight, "I am the greatest!" In today's devotional, we will see that Jesus's take on greatness is vastly different from Muhammed Ali's—and ours if we are honest! Here are Jesus's radical words:

> You know that those who are regarded as rulers of the Gentiles lord it over them, and high officials exercise authority over them. Not so with you. Instead, whoever wants to become great among you must be your servant, and whoever wants to be first must be a slave of all. (Mark 10:42–44)

Background

Jesus and his disciples are approaching Jerusalem. Jesus is leading the way. On the journey from Galilee to Jerusalem, he taught them what it means to be his disciple. He has just made his third prediction of his rejection and condemnation by the Jewish leadership and the mockery, flogging, and death he will experience from the Romans and his resurrection three days later (Mark 10:32–34).

Right after his prediction of his awful suffering and death, James and John approached Jesus, asking him to sit on his right and his left in his glory. Talk about inopportune timing! They obviously did not hear or understand the three predictions of the tragic suffering and death that awaited Jesus in Jerusalem. They were still thinking about the kingdom and about themselves and their status and prestige.

When the other ten disciples heard of this ambitious selfish request, they were indignant with James and John. They were just as ambitious and self-promoting as the brothers! They wanted those special places of power and honor. Pride was in full flow!

Not the first time

This is not the first time that pride has raised its ugly head. Back in Capernaum, after Jesus's second prediction of his rejection, suffering, and death, the disciples started arguing about "who was the greatest." Jesus called them together and said, "Anyone who wants to be first must be the very last, and a servant of all" (Mark 9:35). This sin of pride and the desire to be great, important, respected, and honored above our peers is so powerful! It lives deep within each one of us. It is perhaps the greatest sin (pun intended) because so many other sins follow as we selfishly pursue our pride.

True greatness

This lesson on true greatness is the last lesson Jesus teaches the disciples before he enters Jerusalem and confronts the Jewish leaders. The lesson is so simple to state but so difficult to live out, "Whoever wants to become great among you must be your servant."

Roger's Thesaurus had these synonyms for servant—an assistant, an underling, a subordinate, a hireling, a waiter, an usher, an office boy, a page, a bellboy, a bootblack, a lackey, a stooge, a serf, a vassal, a captive, and a slave. No wonder none of us wants to be a servant! And we haven't even talked about being "a slave of all."

Jesus tells us in the next verse that "the Son of Man did not come to be served but to serve and to give his life a ransom for many." Jesus's actions, not just his words, demonstrated that he was a servant. Just a week after this lesson, he would wash the disciples' feet!

The apostle Paul's favorite title for himself was, "Paul, a servant of Jesus Christ."

I'm third

My sons used to go to a Christian sports camp in Missouri called Kannakuk. It was a four-week camp where the counselors were varsity athletes at some of the major universities. The campers competed fiercely on the fields. But at the end of the camp, the final and most important award was the "I'm third award," Jesus first, others second, and I'm third! The counselors observed the boys over the four weeks and selected the one whose actions demonstrated that he was a servant. Not just a servant heart but servant actions. They were trying to teach the boys that true greatness is not being the best or most competitive athlete but in serving others.

Servants

Ray Pritchard puts the cookies on the bottom shelf, "Servants do whatever needs to be done. They don't wait to be asked. They don't wait to be told. They don't have to be assigned duties. If you are a servant, you don't look at the list to see what you are supposed to do. You just find something to do, and you do it. Servants serve voluntarily on their own initiative."

Let's make this the "year of servanthood." Serving our wives, serving our children, serving our parents and siblings, serving our neighbors, serving our business associates and colleagues, serving our clients and customers, serving our golf buddies, serving the church. Pick one or two of these relationships and make serving this person or persons your prayer and goal for the year.

Being a humble servant is perhaps the distinguishing mark of a true disciple of Jesus.

THE PRICE FOR OUR FREEDOM

Mark 10:45

> For even the Son of Man did not come
> to be served but to serve and to give his life a
> ransom for many. (Mark 10:45)

A great example

Jesus has just instructed his disciples that true greatness comes from being a servant (Mark 10:41–44). He drives home this crucial point by pointing to his own life. It was the life of a servant. About a week later, he would wash his disciple's feet, knowing that one of them would betray him, one of them would deny him three times, and all of them would desert him—all within the next twelve hours! What humility!

Philippians 2:5–8 captures Christ's humility and servant's heart. Although he was fully God, "He made himself nothing by taking the very nature of a servant being made in human likeness, and being found in appearance as a man, he humbled himself by becoming obedient to death—even death on a cross!" He was the Creator, yet he became a created human being. He was omnipotent, yet he was willing to be obedient to death. He was worshipped by angels, yet he allowed himself to be rejected and mocked by evil men! And he did this because he loved us!

What an example of humility and servant behavior!

First John 3:16 applies his example to us: "This is how we know what love is: Jesus laid down his life for us. And we ought to lay down our lives for our brothers." Couldn't be clearer. This is our calling—laying down our lives for our brothers! That's just another way of saying, "Be a servant."

But more than an example

But Jesus laying down his life for us was more than an example of humility and servant behavior. Much more!

On the way from Caesarea Philippi in northern Galilee to Jerusalem Jesus had predicted his suffering, rejection, and death three times to the disciples. But he had not explained why it was necessary for him to die. Now he gives them a cryptic explanation. It is probable that they did not appreciate what it meant at the time. But by the time Mark wrote this Gospel, he understood the significance of Jesus "giving his life a ransom for many," and so would the original Christian readers in Rome.

A ransom

The key word here is *ransom.* It is a term of the marketplace. It means literally "the price of release" and referred in the Roman world of that time to a payment to affect the release of a slave or a captive from bondage. It has inherent in it the concept of substitution. Here in our context, it means that all people are captives under the power of sin and death from which they cannot free themselves. Jesus's substitutionary death paid the price that sets people free. The word *for* is the Greek word *anti*, which here means "instead of" or "in place of." This reinforces the idea of substitution. So Jesus is predicting to his disciples that not only will he suffer, be rejected, and die, but also that his death would pay the price or penalty for sin instead of them paying the price or penalty for their sins and that he will set free those who would believe in him.

Substitution

The concept of animal sacrifices in the Old Testament Jewish worship system is behind these words. Every morning and every evening, a burnt offering was made in the temple. The animal had to be healthy and unblemished—representing the perfectness of the sacrifice. The offeree (the sinner) would lay his hand on the head of the animal—symbolizing that his sin was being transferred to the animal and that the animal's "perfectness" was being transferred to him. Then the animal (now symbolically bearing the sin of the offeree) was killed instead of or in the place of the offeree. The animal bore the judgment for sin (which was death) as a substitute for the sinful offeree. The sinful offeree's sin was atoned for, and he could go free bearing symbolically the perfectness of the animal.

The servant song of Isaiah 53 is likely also behind the word *ransom*. "He was pierced for our transgressions, he was crushed for our iniquities, and the punishment that brought us peace was on him, and by his wounds we are healed" (vs. 5). Jesus, the Servant, was pierced instead of us, he was crushed instead of us, he was punished instead of us, and he was wounded instead of us! In his death, he paid for our transgressions, iniquities, and punishment instead of us paying for them. This is what it means that he "gave his life a ransom for many." The "many" are those who would believe that he was their substitute—that he paid the ransom price (his death) to set us free.

Freedom

The word *ransom* and the related *lutr-* word group always has two ideas: the payment of the price and the resulting freedom or deliverance of the one for whom the price was paid. Sometimes the context emphasizes the price paid (Christ's death) and sometimes the emphasis is on the deliverance or freedom of the one for whom the price was paid. Here both are equally emphasized.

We are set free from the consequences and penalty of our sin—spiritual and eternal death. We are set free from guilt. We are set free from a meaningless life. We are set free from legalism—trying to earn our way to heaven through our own measly "payments." Jesus paid it all!

Takeaway

Because of God's amazing grace, I am totally forgiven—past, present, and future. I have been declared to be not guilty of my sins. I have been declared to be forever righteous—having received Christ's imputed perfectness (righteousness). I am fully ransomed. I am so unworthy but so thankful.

Enjoy your freedom in Christ. Revel in God's grace and Jesus's fully paid ransom and lay down your lives for your brothers!

CHAPTER 13

THE NON-TRIUMPHAL ENTRY

Mark 11:1–11

> When they brought the colt to Jesus and threw their clothes over it, he sat on it. Many people spread their cloaks in the road, while others spread branches they had cut from the fields. Those who went ahead and those who followed shouted, "Hosanna!" "Blessed is he who comes in the name of the Lord!" "Blessed is the coming kingdom of our father David!" "Hosanna in the highest!" (Mark 11:7–11)

Jesus's entry into Jerusalem is the "official" presentation of himself as the promised Messiah. It is accompanied by praise and acceptance by his followers but is met with indifference and rejection by the religious leaders and the inhabitants of Jerusalem.

Flashback

Jesus began his public ministry, proclaiming, "The time has come, the kingdom of God is near, repent and believe the good news" (Mark 1:14–15). This was true because the King (the incarnate Messiah Jesus) had arrived. He backed up his claim with miracles and powerful authoritative teaching. But the Jewish religious leaders soon opposed Him, and by chapter 3, they were plotting to kill him and derisively attributed his miracles to the power of Beelzebub (Satan). So Jesus then turned his focus primarily to his disciples who in chapter 8 finally confess, "You are the Christ (Messiah)" (Mark 8:29). Jesus then concentrates on teaching his believing disciples in preparation for his departure as they move slowly to Jerusalem.

The entry

Jesus entered his city, Jerusalem, and headed to his temple in a prophetic WAY, with a prophetic ANNOUNCEMENT, and on a prophetic DAY.

He came riding on a colt (identified as a donkey in Luke's Gospel) in fulfillment of Zechariah 9:9, "Rejoice greatly, O Daughter of Zion! Shout, Daughter of Jerusalem! See you king comes to you, righteous and having salvation, gentle and riding on a donkey, on a colt, the foal of a donkey."

His followers shouting, "Hosanna," which means "save," was an announcement to Jerusalem that salvation (in the person of Jesus the Messiah) was entering Jerusalem. The announcement was clear, "Blessed is he who comes in the name of the Lord! Blessed in the coming kingdom of our father David." His followers announced to the city of Jerusalem that this Jesus was the Messiah, the promised descendant of David, the Eternal

King promised to Israel, and perhaps expected him to continue into Jerusalem and the temple and set up his promised kingdom.

And according to Dr. Harold Hoehner in his book *Chronological Aspects in the Life of Christ*, Jesus's entry in Jerusalem (which he dates as March 30, AD 33) took place on a prophetic day—exactly 483 sabbatical years (173,880 days) after "the issuing of the decree to restore and rebuild Jerusalem" (March 5, 444 BC) as prophesied in Daniel 9:25.

The response of the city

Jesus's entry into Jerusalem could have been (should have been) a great day of rejoicing. The fulfillment of a thousand years of prophecy. This is the "official" (in the sense that it fulfills Old Testament prophesy) announcement and presentation of Jesus as the Messiah to the nation of Israel. He was offering them the promised Davidic kingdom of peace, prosperity, and spiritual blessings. But the Jewish inhabitants of Jerusalem would not "repent and believe," the prerequisite to the inauguration of the Davidic kingdom. The city of Jerusalem, full of pilgrims, getting ready to celebrate Passover, rejected him. Actually, it was worse—they ignored Him. Verse 11 is one of the saddest verses in the Bible: "Jesus entered Jerusalem and went to the temple. He looked around at everything, but since it was already late, he went out to Bethany with the twelve."

The Messianic King had entered his city and came to his temple—and nobody cared!

Disappointing reality

His faithful followers who announced his Messianic entry into Jerusalem were no doubt disappointed that the city as a whole went about their business as though the Messiah was not there. The "real" Lamb of God was riding into the city, but they were busy choosing their Passover lambs and so completely missed it.

But this is the reality that we believers face. In spite of what seems to us as overwhelming evidence that Jesus is the Messiah, the God-Man, the world around us operates as though he does not exist. Worse than rejecting him, they ignore him, just like the city of Jerusalem on that Palm Sunday.

Encouraging reality

But in spite of the world's response to Jesus, we know that he is indeed the Messiah promised in the Old Testament. He did die on the cross for our sins, and he rose again and is now at the right hand of the Father. He has forgiven our sins, given us the gift of his spirit, and promised to never leave or forsake us no matter how hard the journey. And one day, he is coming again to the earth to set up his kingdom of peace, prosperity, security, and blessing. Then everyone will recognize that Jesus is the Messiah. Every knee will bow, and every tongue will confess that Jesus the Messiah is Lord (Philippians 2:10). On that day, he will not be ignored! In the meanwhile, be faithful, patient, and persevere.

CHAPTER 14

CONDEMNATION OF THE TEMPLE

Mark 11:12–25

On reaching Jerusalem, Jesus entered the temple courts and began to throw out those who were buying and selling there. He overturned the tables of the money changers and the benches of those selling doves, and would not allow anyone to carry merchandise through the temple courts. As he taught them, he said "Is it not written: 'My house will be called a house of prayer for all nations'? But you have made if a den of robbers.'" (Mark 11:15–17)

Jesus condemns and predicts judgment on the corrupt Jewish temple and its practices and reveals the new way of praying with faith directly to God.

Quick overview of Mark 11:12–25

This is Monday morning of the Passion week. Jesus sees a fig tree outside of Jerusalem and curses it for having plenty of leaves but no figs for him to eat. He then enters the temple and disrupts their crooked money-changing and selling of sacrificial animals and birds. This infuriated the chief priests and the teachers of the law who were looking for a way to kill Jesus. On the way out of Jerusalem, the disciples see the fig tree withered from its roots. This amazed and concerned the disciples. Jesus responded by teaching about the need to trust God and how to pray to him.

Condemnation of the temple religious system

Some people refer to this as the "cleansing of the temple." But Jesus was not trying to reform the corrupt temple worship practices. After all, the tables and booths would be up and back in business in a day or two. No, this was a symbolic and prophetic act that powerfully condemned and predicted future judgment on the whole corrupt temple system. The temple was the heart of the Covenant that God made with Moses at Mount Sinai back in 1440 BC after the exodus from Egypt. It was there that God's presence dwelt, it was there that the Israelites worshipped and prayed, this was where the law was taught. The temple was the visible sign of their unique relationship with God. Herod's temple was a magnificent building (one of the original seven wonders of the world). But after hundreds of years of corruption and rebellion, God was finally saying enough!

Judgment on the temple

The fig tree is a familiar symbol for the nation of Israel in the Old Testament, and here it serves as an object lesson to the disciples. All show but no spiritual fruit! In spite of its outward rituals, the temple religious system is irredeemably corrupt and sinful. Jesus is in effect cursing it and predicting that it will die from the inside out like the cursed fig tree. The temple stood for the Mosaic Covenant, so Jesus was predicting two things. One, the Mosaic Covenant (which was the legal and religious "constitution" of the nation of Israel) would be annulled and be replaced by the New Covenant (which happened on the day of Pentecost, about fifty-five days hence). Two, that the temple (and the city of Jerusalem) would be destroyed, which happened in AD 70.

Prayers of faith

The disciples grasped to some degree that Jesus was predicting the demise of the temple, so their obvious concern was: how then do we worship and pray to God if there are no priests and no temple? And remember the temple was intended to be a "house of prayer." So Jesus's teaching here is in response to their concern. First, he states, "Have faith in God," and not the temple! And second, under the coming New Covenant, you can worship and pray directly to God without the mediation of the priests or the temple.

But in addition, he holds out this amazing promise:

> Truly I tell you, if anyone says to this
> mountain, "go throw yourself into the sea,
> and does not doubt in their heart but believes
> that what they say will happen, it will be done

for them. Therefore, I tell you, whatever you ask for in prayer, believe that you have it, and it will be yours." (vss. 23–24)

Application

This promise is no doubt conditioned on praying for things that are in God's will (not Ferraris and mansions). But as I studied this promise this week, I made a prayer list of four things that I believe are likely to be his will (family, ministry, and future) and am committed to praying for them in faith. Perhaps God might nudge you to do the same.

CHAPTER 15

GIVE TO CAESAR WHAT BELONGS TO CAESAR AND TO GOD WHAT BELONGS TO GOD

Mark 12:13–37

Quick overview of Mark 12:13–37. It's still Tuesday of the Passion Week. The confrontation between Jesus and the Jewish religious leaders is escalating. This section is structured around four questions. The first two, regarding whether to pay taxes to Caesar or not, and the gag question from the Sadducees about the resurrection, are designed to trap Jesus into saying something that would give the religious leaders (or the Romans) a reason to arrest him. The third question about the greatest commandment is a genuine question that Jesus answers in the same positive spirit (Mark 12:28–34). The fourth question is posed by Jesus himself and makes the point that Jesus is both David's Son and David's Lord (Mark 12:35–37).

We will look at the first question.

After some hypocritical flattery certain Pharisees and Herodians asked him this question to trap him: "Is it right to pay the imperial tax to Caesar or not? Should we pay or shouldn't we?" (Mark 12:14–15).

The issue

The "imperial tax" was the annual poll tax (head tax) demanded by the Roman Emperor from Jews since AD 6 when Judea became a Roman province. The money went straight into the emperor's treasury. The Jews hated this tax because it reminded them of their subjugation to Rome.

The question was a trick question. If he answered yes, he would antagonize the Jewish people—no one claiming to be the Messiah would sanction the willing submission of God's chosen people to pagan rulers. If he answered no, the religious leaders could go to Pilate and turn Jesus in as an insurrectionist.

The coin

Jesus asked them to bring him a *denarius*, which was a small silver coin and was the only coin acceptable to pay the imperial tax. Taking the coin, he set up his answer with this question: "Whose image is this? And whose inscription?" They replied, "Caesar's."

In fact, the image was probably of Tiberius Caesar and the inscription read in Latin, "Tiberius Caesar Augustus, Son of the Divine Augustus" and on the back side, "Chief Priest." This inscription originated in the imperial cult of emperor worship and was clearly a claim to divinity. You can see why this was so repulsive to the Jews!

Jesus's answer

"Give back to Caesar what belongs to Caesar, and to God what belongs to God" is his answer. He skillfully avoided the trap by turning the either/or question into a both/and answer. But what exactly did he mean?

In spite of its repulsive image and inscription, paying the imperial tax acknowledged that Rome did have civil and political authority over Judea. And there were certain civil benefits of the "Pax Romana" (roads, travel, commerce, efficient civil administration, peace, etc.) that the Jews enjoyed under Rome's rule.

Paying the imperial tax acknowledged that Rome had an appropriate sphere of both civil responsibility and authority that needed to be honored and respected. So his first point is that they should pay the required tax to Rome AND honor God.

Main point

But it is the second half of that answer, "(Give) to God what belongs to God," that is Jesus's main point. While it is possible that Jesus was referring to paying the temple tax that each Jew was instructed to pay, more likely he is challenging the emperor's claim to deity. The emperor had limited civil authority, but he was not to receive the divine honor and worship he claimed. God's people are "God's coins" in that they bear his image (Genesis 1:27). They owe him what belongs to him— their total allegiance to Him as the one true God, the Creator of everything.

This is a crucial issue to Jesus.

Application

Since I filed an extension back in April, earlier this week, I met with my accountant to finalize our taxes. Like most of you (and the Jews of Jesus's day), I think my taxes are unfair and way too high. And I don't agree with how much of it is spent. But unfortunately, I was studying this passage and was reminded of Jesus's *command* to "give to Uncle Sam and the State of California all that rightfully belongs to them under the current laws" (my paraphrase). No fudging! With integrity! Romans 13:7 also came to mind: "If you owe taxes, pay taxes."

However, the main thrust of Jesus's clever answer is: Do not get all worked up on lesser matters like arguably unfair taxes. Instead, focus on the main thing. We are to give our total allegiance to the one true God. We bear his image (although scarred and flawed). We belong to him. His Son, Jesus, died and rose again to give us the gift of eternal life. He wants our total commitment. To use Jesus's words later in the chapter we are to:

> Love (give loyal and sacrificial commitment to) the Lord your God, with all your heart and with all your soul and with all your mind and with all your strength. (Mark 12:30)

TOTAL COMMITMENT TO GOD

Mark 12:38–44

Summary of Mark 12:38–44. This section concludes Jesus's public ministry and his confrontation with the religious leaders. In the first paragraph (Mark 12:38–40), he denounces the teachers of the law for their ostentatious conduct, greed, and hypocrisy. By way of contrast, Mark then records the account that we know as the "widow's mite." The widow's humble, sacrificial gift evidenced her total and genuine commitment to her Lord. Two polar opposites.

Jesus condemns the hypocrisy of the Jewish teachers of the law

The Jewish teachers of the law (called scribes in older translations) wore long white linen robes with tassels at the bottom. Their white clothes were a mark of distinction that set them apart from ordinary people. Because they taught the law and thus spoke for God, the majority of the people venerated them and treated them with respect and even awe. But the teachers of the law in Jesus's day had, for the most part, lost their way spiritually and were abusing their esteemed position. Jesus warned, "Watch out for the teachers of the law. They like to walk around in flowing robes and be greeted with respect in the marketplaces and have the most important seats in the synagogues and the places of honor at banquets." What an arrogant, pompous self-glorifying bunch!

Because they got no pay for their services, they depended on the hospitality of many devout Jews. But they often abused this hospitality. The phrase "they devour widows' houses" is a vivid figure of speech for how they exploited the generosity of people of limited means, especially widows, often unethically appropriating their property and resources—in the name of God, of course! And to make it worse "for a show they make lengthy prayers." They were religious hustlers. They would have made great TV evangelists! But above everything they were hypocrites, and Jesus hated religious hypocrisy.

Humility

Mark's point is that God and Jesus want the exact opposite from a true disciple. Someone who does not need to look special, who does not seek personal accolades, who is happy with the less important roles in church and at social functions, and who humbly helps the weak and poor. God is interested in the heart, in genuine spirituality, which looks a lot like Paul's words in Philippians 2:3–4, "Do nothing out of selfish ambition or vain conceit. Rather, in humility value others above yourselves, not looking on your own interests but each of you the interests of others."

Jesus commends the humble sacrifice of the widow's gift

Against the wall of the women's court in the temple there were thirteen trumpet-shaped collection receptacles for receiving the worshippers' offerings and contributions. Jesus sat opposite one of these receptacles observing how the Passover crowd was putting their money into the temple treasury. In contrast to many wealthy people who gave large amounts, an unnamed "poor widow came and put in two very small copper coins, worth only a few cents."

> Calling his disciples to him, Jesus said, "Truly I tell you, this poor widow has put more into the treasury than all the others. They gave out of their wealth; but she out of her poverty put in everything—all she had to live on." (Mark 12:42–44)

She could have held back one of the coins for herself. But instead, she gave all she had to live on. In giving to God so sacrificially she completely entrusted herself to God to provide for her needs. Jesus is clearly using her as an example to teach his disciples (and us) the value God places on wholehearted commitment.

Also, notice that her gift was not made ostentatiously looking for accolades for her gift. If Jesus had not singled her out, no one would have noticed her among the Passover crowd, and that's how her humble heart wanted it. It was a gift to God "made in secret." But Jesus who sees the heart behind the action, saw her humble sacrificial gift as a further example to us to serve, and give our gifts and contributions humbly and sacrificially and "in secret," the exact opposite of the pompous, ostentatious actions of the teachers of the law.

Takeaway

Maybe this week you could do one sacrificial act or give one sacrificial gift "in secret," one that no one knows about except you and God, and perhaps the recipient. Jesus would like that.

The message to the disciples from the extended teaching of Jesus in the synagogue is a call to total commitment and absolute surrender to God.

BE FAITHFUL AND STEADFAST IN THE MIDST OF CALAMITY

Mark 13:1–36

The disciples' question. As Jesus was leaving the temple, one of his disciples commented: "Look teacher! What massive stones! What magnificent buildings!" (vs. 1). Jesus replied with this amazing prediction: "Not one stone will here will be left on another; all will be thrown down" (vs. 2).

Having only the perspective of the Old Testament (e.g. Zechariah 14), the disciples assumed that the destruction of the temple and the city of Jerusalem was part of God's purging and judgment that would end this present age and would inaugurate the promised Messianic Kingdom. So their follow-up question indicates that they were thinking that the destruction of the temple and the final judgment would happen at the same time:

> Tell us when will these things happen.
> And what will be the sign that they are all
> about to be fulfilled? (vs. 4)

Jesus's answer

Jesus's answer (vss. 5–37) is usually referred to as the Olivet Discourse (because it took place on the Mount of Olives). While his answer is a little difficult to follow, he seems to first state that many events will occur before the destruction of Jerusalem, and when it is destroyed, it will be a time of great suffering and distress—as God judges the disobedient and rebellious nation of Israel. Then he indicates that a similar time of distress and judgment will precede His return to the earth. The heart and climax of the discourse is:

> But in those days following the distress,
> "the sun will be darkened, and the moon will
> not give its light; the stars will fall from the sky,
> and the heavenly bodies will be shaken." At
> that time people will see the Son of Man com-
> ing in the clouds with great power and glory.
> And he will send his angels and gather his elect
> from the four winds, form the ends of the
> earth to the ends of the heavens. (vss.24–27)

What we learn from Jesus's answer

Four things seem to stand out from Jesus's answer. First, there will be much activity and time between his prophecy (about AD 33), and the destruction of the temple and city (which happened in AD 70), and again between the destruction of the temple and his return (still future!). Second, before both the destruction of the temple and the return of Christ, there will be times of great distress, suffering, and calamity. Believers will suffer and be persecuted. Third, Jesus promises that believers who are caught up in these challenging times will be supernaturally empowered by the Holy Spirit. Fourth, all suffering, persecution, and tribulation will cease when he returns in power and glory—and faithful believers will in included in his glory and future Messianic kingdom.

The main point of Jesus's answer

The point of Jesus's answer is not to encourage us and look for signs of his coming or to set out a chronology of future events. Rather, the thrust of Jesus's answer is found in his concluding words:

> But about that day or hour no one
> knows, not even the angels in heaven, nor the
> Son, but only the Father. Be on your guard!
> Be alert! You do not know when that time
> will come. (vs. 32)

The punchline to the last parable in chapter 13 (the parable of the absent owner) is:

> Therefore keep watch because you
> do not know when the owner of the house
> (Jesus) will come back. (vs. 35)

Jesus is not primarily instructing his disciples (and by extension Mark's original readers and us) to watch for his return—although other passages do instruct us to wait expectantly for his return. Rather, the burden of this passage is a call to be faithful on his behalf while he is away—to be steadfast and tenacious through often difficult times.

Specifically, in this discourse, we are encouraged to be courageous despite turmoil in the world (vss. 7–8) and natural disasters (vs. 8), to stand firm when under persecution (vs. 9), to continue in the proclamation of the gospel (vs. 10), to be unshaken despite betrayal from those close to us (vs. 12), to refuse to be misled (vss. 6, 21–22), and so on.

Takeaway

Trials, suffering, distress, and calamity are a part of life—the prosperity gospel notwithstanding! Mark's point to his readers is: No matter what era you are living in, no matter how fierce the opposition, how difficult the trial, how deep the distress, or how seemingly out of control and turbulent national and world events around us are, the disciple of Jesus is to be alert, steadfast, and faithful to Jesus. Jesus's promise is that the Holy Spirit will supernaturally aid us through the difficult times (vs. 11), and most significantly, one day he will return in power and glory and deliver us from this fallen messed-up world when he sets up his kingdom in the new heaven and earth (vs. 26–27). And we will be there with him!

So be alert and faithful. Don't despair. Don't give in to negativity and pessimism. One day "the kingdom of this world will become the kingdom of our Lord and Christ" (Revelation 11:15). We know how the story ends!

THE RESURRECTION CHANGES EVERYTHING

Mark 14 and 15

Overview of Mark 14–15. On a first read, these two chapters seem pretty morbid. The Jewish leaders are "scheming to arrest and secretly kill Jesus" (Mark 14:1–2). A woman anoints Jesus "to prepare for his burial" (Mark 14:3–9). Judas Iscariot agrees to betray Jesus (Mark 14:10–11). At the Last Supper, Jesus says to his disciples, "One of you will betray me, one who is eating with me," which put a pall over their Passover meal (Mark 14:12–28). Jesus predicts that Peter will deny him three times (Mark 14:29–31). In the garden of Gethsemane, Jesus "deeply distressed and troubled" wrestles in prayer with the Father regarding his imminent death (Mark 14:32–42). Jesus is arrested and his disciples "deserted him and fled" (Mark 14:43–52). Jesus is tried before the Sanhedrin and falsely convicted of blasphemy (Mark 14:53–65). Peter denies Jesus three times (Mark 14:66–72). Jesus is hurriedly tried before Pilate who gives in to the Jewish religious leaders and "has Jesus flogged, and handed him over to be crucified" (Mark 15:1–15). Jesus is mocked and humiliated by the Roman soldiers (Mark 15:16–20), taken to Golgotha and crucified (Mark 15:21–41), and then hastily buried by Joseph of Arimathea.

It looks like Jesus is losing at every turn and that Satan and evil are winning. He appears to be helplessly caught up in the swift current of events orchestrated by the jealous and vindictive Jewish religious leaders. It seems that God and Jesus have lost control. Nothing is going right!

The resurrection perspective

But the resurrection changed everything. Mark's original readers in Rome knew the "rest of the story" and would have read these events through the lens of the resurrection. And so do we. Christ's resurrection makes sense of these events. We learn that in spite of what seems to be the triumph of evil, God is actually orchestrating the events to accomplish his will and purposes. Peter in his great sermon on the Day of Pentecost makes this so clear:

> This man (Jesus) was handed over to you by God's deliberate plan and foreknowledge; and you (Jewish people), with the help of wicked men, put him to death by nailing him to a cross. But God raised him from the dead… (Acts 2:23–24)

What appeared to be the greatest miscarriage of justice was, in fact, from the perspective of the resurrection, the greatest moment in the history of mankind. God was using the tragic and unjust events recorded in these chapters to accomplish his will and purpose, which was for Jesus to die on the cross. Jesus's death on the cross, of course, paid for our sins, defeated sin and Satan, and provided a way for us to be forgiven, reconciled to God, and given the gift of eternal life. Without Christ's unjust death on the cross, these eternal blessings would not be available to us. God was in control all the time. The resurrection proves this.

God is in control

Some of you reading this may be going through a period where everything seems to be going wrong. Perhaps it's your job or career that is just flatlining, your marriage that is on life support, your kids that don't want to embrace your family's values, aged parents that are exhausting, or your (or your family's) health is failing. Or maybe you have made some decisions or taken some actions that are at best unwise or at worst seriously sinful. And to make it worse, your desperate prayers don't seem to reach God. Not to mention our politically divided country (the USA), which seems to have abandoned its Christian roots and sometimes seems to be hurtling toward disaster.

But the resurrection yells out to us that God is, in fact, in control and is superintending events in our lives (both individually and nationally) to accomplish his purposes. We may never discover WHY God allowed these things to happen to us. But on that great Resurrection Day when Christ returns, we will see clearly how and why he was using every event in our lives for his glory and our good. But until then, we just need to trust him.

Takeaway

Christ's resurrection and our certain future resurrection provide encouragement and hope in our dark times. God is gracious, loving, and good, and we know that "in all things, God works for the good of those who love him, who have been called according to his purpose" (Romans 8:28). No matter how bleak or tragic our world appears, God is orchestrating the circumstances and events of our lives for his will and purposes, and for our good. He is in control ALL the time. The resurrection proves that.

CHAPTER 19

THE LORD'S SUPPER

Mark 14:12–26

Summary of Mark 14:12–26. On Thursday of the Passion Week, Jesus sent two of his disciples to the city of Jerusalem to prepare the Passover meal. A large upstairs guest room was made available to Jesus where the two disciples prepared the Passover meal. Jesus arrived with "the Twelve" that evening—probably about 6:00 p.m. since the fifteenth on Nisan (Passover Day) started at 6:00 p.m.—and he and his disciples reclined at the table.

The Passover meal was full of symbolism. The head of the household would remind those present how each part of the meal (including the breaking of bread and the drinking of wine) looked back to some aspect of Israel's deliverance from Egypt. Jesus, however, changed the symbolism of the Old Covenant and created new symbolism that looked to the New Covenant, thereby indicating that the Old Covenant was being abolished and the New Covenant was about to be inaugurated.

The two elements

The Passover meal had many symbols, but Jesus focused on just two—the bread and the wine. These are the symbols of the New Covenant.

The bread

> While they were eating, Jesus took bread, and when he had given thanks, he broke it and gave it to his disciples, saying, "Take it; this is my body." (Mark 14:22)

Luke adds what is implied in Mark, "which is given for you." The apostle Paul, in giving the longest description of the Lord's Supper, likewise adds, "Which is for you."

The bread is a symbol or signpost that points to Jesus's body, which was given to us. "Body" does not just mean his physical body; rather, it is a figure of speech (a metonymy) that means his whole Person. Jesus's whole person was given to us. He, the perfect Man, gave himself for us. He took our sins upon himself. He stood in our place. The bread points to the truth that he was our substitute.

The wine

Regarding the cup of wine, Jesus said, "This is my blood of the covenant, which is poured out for many" (Mark 14:24). Matthew's Gospel adds, "For the forgiveness of sins," and Luke clarifies that the "covenant" Jesus refers to is the "New Covenant."

"Blood" is a metaphor for "violent death." His violent death refers not just to his physical agony on the cross, but more to the awful agony of experiencing the holy and just wrath of God as payment for our sins. So the cup is a symbol of Jesus's violent death on the cross that inaugurates the New Covenant. The two key blessings of the New Covenant are the forgiveness of sins and the indwelling of the Holy Spirit.

Do this in remembrance of Me

The bread and the wine are symbols that together point to Christ's violent death on the cross as our substitute.

The apostle Paul, in setting out the practice of the Lord's Supper in the early church, records Jesus's words, which give us the purpose of the Lord's Supper: "Do this in remembrance of Me" (1 Corinthians 11:24–25). Paul also adds that "whenever you eat this bread and drink this cup, you proclaim the Lord's death until he comes" (vs. 26).

Next time you partake of the Lord's Supper, deeply reflect and remember his once-and-for-all death on the cross as our substitute. He died the death that I deserved to die. It is a tangible reminder that through faith in his death, I can experience the blessings of the New Covenant—forgiveness of sins and the gift of the Holy Spirit. The Lord's Supper is characterized by gratitude and thanksgiving for Christ's death and what it has accomplished for us.

Takeaway

Every day we are attacked and tempted by the world, the flesh, and the devil. And the reality is that we stumble and sin a lot more than we care to admit. We are in constant need of forgiveness! The bread and the wine, which we can see, touch, taste, and smell are concrete symbols that Christ's death on the cross was "for the forgiveness of sins." The forgiveness of my sins! Communion is for sinners like us. It drives us back to the essence of the gospel: "Christ died for our sins according to the Scriptures" (1 Corinthians 15:3).

Communion is also a time of worship and communion with God. Communion is not something we do alone; there is an important horizontal aspect to Communion as we share the experience of remembrance and worship with our fellow believers. We together proclaim the Lord's death.

And Christians will continue to celebrate the Lord's Supper "until he comes." This is the great "certain expectation" (hope) of all Christians. One day, Jesus will return to set up his kingdom.

CHAPTER 20

PETER'S FAILURES AND RESTORATION

Mark 14:27–72

Mark's Gospel is likely the apostle Peter's account of the life of Jesus as told to and recorded by Mark. So it is interesting to read how honest and candid Mark (Peter) is about Peter's embarrassing failures. This is seen especially in Mark 14.

Peter's boast (Mark 14:27–31)

Late Thursday night, on the way from the Upper Room in the city of Jerusalem to the Garden of Gethsemane, Jesus predicted that the disciples would "all fall away" when he was arrested. In response, Peter boldly declared, "Even if all fall away, I will not."

Jesus responds to Peter's proud boast by predicting that Peter will disown Jesus before the rooster crowed the next morning. Peter raises the ante with this even more emphatic declaration: "Even if I have to die with you, I will never disown you."

There is no doubt that in spite of his self-righteous stinking pride, Peter really meant it at the time. But, of course, pride goes before a fall.

Peter's failures (Mark 14:32–72)

When Jesus and his disciples arrive at Gethsemane, Jesus takes Peter, James, and John with him a short distance from the others where Jesus agonized in prayer in anticipation of his imminent crucifixion. He asked them to "watch and pray" with him in his hour of distress. But when Jesus came back to them, he found them fast asleep. He directed his disappointment at Peter (no doubt as a reminder of Peter's bold boast a few hours earlier), saying, "Simon, are you asleep? Couldn't you keep watch for one hour?" Twice more Jesus went away to pray, and each time he came back and found Peter, James, and John asleep!

When Jesus is arrested a short time later, "Everyone deserted him and fled" (Mark 14:50), just as Jesus had predicted. And Peter, in spite of his bold words, fled too.

During Jesus's trial before the Sanhedrin later that night (or rather early Friday morning), Peter infamously disowns Jesus three times. Exactly as Jesus had predicted! Interestingly, his first two denials were to a "servant girl" who thought she identified him as being with Jesus. I wonder if that challenge had come from a man, whether Peter would not have courageously stood up and confessed that he was a disciple of Jesus. But a "girl," maybe good-looking, is often the innocent tool of Satan. We men have such a weakness in this area. So many of our "denials" of Jesus (whether in words, thoughts, or actions) are related to an attractive female. Enough said!

Peter's repentance, forgiveness, and restoration

Immediately after his third denial, Peter remembered Jesus's prediction, and "he broke down and wept." Along with his grief and self-recrimination, there was repentance. Humbled at his earlier proud declarations, he no doubt acknowledged his pride and sinfulness. This a place familiar to all of us.

Three days later, the angel at the empty tomb announced to the three women who had come to anoint Jesus's body that Jesus had risen from the dead. Then he added, "But go, tell his disciples AND PETER, 'He is going ahead of you into Galilee. There you will see him, just as he told you.'" Peter is specially singled out by the angel (speaking for God). Yes, this Peter who fell asleep, who fled, and who denied Jesus—in spite of his boastful words to the contrary. Yes, God wanted to make sure that this Peter went to Galilee to see the resurrected Jesus.

Then we all remember that great episode recorded in the twenty-first chapter of John's Gospel. After serving breakfast, Jesus takes Peter aside and gently restores him to leadership among the disciples. Three times (clearly to correspond to the three denials) Jesus asks him whether he is loyally committed to him. Peter reaffirms his commitment to Jesus. Jesus not only restores Peter, but he also recommissions his with the thrice repeated, "Feed my sheep."

Peter, fully forgiven, restored, and recommissioned, becomes the leader of the early church, preaching that great sermon of the day of Pentecost and courageously standing for Jesus in spite of fierce persecution.

Takeaway

We have all made bold (and perhaps proud and presumptuous) commitments to God. To be morally pure, have financial integrity, abstain from pornography, alcohol, swearing, losing temper, overeating, etc. To read the Bible every day, to pray with our wives, to have family devotions, to witness to our business associates, to give more sacrificially, and so on. And at the time we really meant it. But the pull of the world, the flesh, and the devil are powerful. And like Peter, we often fail and fall. Sometimes spectacularly.

But the good news is that if we, like Peter, repent and recommit, God in his grace will forgive and restore. He is the God of second chances and third, and fourth and… And in his grace, he not only forgives and restores, but also he recommissions us to powerfully serve him.

God is not finished with you yet. No matter how badly you have failed and fallen, like Peter, there is forgiveness, restoration, and even meaningful service in your future.

God's amazing grace!

CHAPTER 21

RELIGIOUS TRIAL BEFORE THE SANHEDRIN

Mark 14:53–65

> Again, the high priest asked him, "Are you the Messiah, the Son of the Blessed One?" "I am," said Jesus. "And you will see the Son of Man sitting at the right hand of the Mighty One and coming on the clouds of heaven." (Mark 14: 61–62)

Backdrop

Late Thursday night, Jesus had been arrested in the Garden of Gethsemane (betrayed by Judas) and was taken before the Jewish high priest, whose name was Caiaphas. The Sanhedrin was hastily convened. The Sanhedrin was the Jewish Leadership Council and consisted of seventy-one representatives, plus the high priest. Twice they tried to get witnesses to testify against Jesus, but the witnesses and their false testimony did not agree. But the Sanhedrin was determined to convict Jesus and put him to death. Finally, the high priest in desperation asked Jesus the key question, "Are you the Messiah, the Son of the Blessed One"?

Jesus's short answer

Jesus's initial answer is clear and unequivocal: "I am." In Mark's Gospel up to this point, Jesus has consistently told his disciples and would-be disciples not to publicly announce that he is the Messiah. This is sometimes referred to by scholars as "the Messianic secret." That is, Jesus's desire to keep his identity secret from the religious leaders and authorities until the right time. Well, this was now the right time! Jesus's claim is crystal clear. He is claiming to be the Messiah in front of the High Priest and the Sanhedrin.

The longer answer

But Jesus's answer goes much further. He further announces that he is "the Son of Man" in such a way that identifies him with two Old Testament scriptures that all the Sanhedrin would know well.

Daniel 7:13–14

In Daniel 7, Daniel had a vision in which he saw "one like a son of man, coming in the clouds of heaven" and being led into the presence of the "Ancient of Days" (clearly Yahweh himself). Then this "Son of Man" is given everlasting God-like kingly power:

> He (the Son of Man) was given author-
> ity, glory and sovereign power; all nations

and peoples of every language worshipped him. His dominion is an everlasting dominion that will not pass away, and his kingdom will never be destroyed. (Daniel 7:14).

Jesus's continued answer, "And you will see the Son of Man sitting at the right hand of the Mighty One and coming on the clouds on heaven" was clearly intended to say: I am the "Son of Man" that Daniel saw in his vision. I will one day be given this glory and power. I will one day be worshipped by "all nations and peoples." And I will one day set up an everlasting kingdom "that will never be destroyed."

You can see why this freaked the high priest out. Jesus was not only claiming to be the Messiah but also was clearly claiming to be God!

Psalm 110

The other Scripture Jesus alludes to is Psalm 110. The familiar first verse reads:

> The Lord said to my Lord: Sit at my right hand until I make your enemies a footstool for your feet.

Jesus had earlier (in Mark 13: 35–37) identified himself as the second "Lord" referred to in this verse. The psalm goes on to describe the godlike kingly power and splendor of this "Lord" who sits at Yahweh's right hand and particularly his decisive judgment of his enemies.

Again, Jesus is saying, "I am Lord and will one day judge you along with all my enemies when I return to establish my eternal kingdom."

Jesus is Messiah and Lord

Jesus appears so weak and vulnerable before these Jewish religious leaders. They condemned him to death for his blasphemous words. They spit on him and beat him. Shortly they will take him to Pilate who would authorize his crucifixion. But outward appearances and circumstances are often deceiving!

In fact, this Jesus, this Son of Man, is indeed not only the Messiah but also God in the flesh! After Jesus's resurrection and ascension to "the right hand of God," the apostle Peter in his sermon on the Day of Pentecost quotes Psalm 110:1 and then concludes his sermon with these words:

> Therefore, let all Israel be assured of this: God has made this Jesus, whom you crucified, both Lord and Christ (Messiah). (Acts 2:36)

Of course, one day he is coming back to earth to fulfill Daniel's prophesy and Psalm 110, judging his enemies and establishing his glorious and eternal kingdom. At that time, "all nations and peoples of every language" will worship him as Messiah and Lord. This includes the high priest and Sanhedrin who condemned him to death. This includes the scoffers of our day as well.

Takeaway

Jesus clearly claimed to be both Messiah and God. As C. S. Lewis commented: he is either a liar, a lunatic, or what he claimed to be—the Messiah and God in the flesh. There are really no other options. And since he is indeed Messiah and Lord, we owe him our worship and wholehearted commitment.

THE CRUCIFIXION OF JESUS

Mark 15:6–41

> At noon darkness came over the whole land until three in the afternoon. And at three in the afternoon, Jesus cried out in a loud voice, "Eloi, Eloi. Lema Sabachthani?" (which means "My God, my God, why have you forsaken me?)" (Mark 15:33–34)

Overview of the Crucifixion

The Roman prefect Pilate released Barabbas, had Jesus flogged, and then handed him over to the Roman soldiers to crucify him. The soldiers put a purple robe on him, twisted together a crown of thorns that they placed on his head, and then proceeded to pay mocking homage to him calling out to him "Hail, king of the Jews" and hitting him on the head. After they had had their cruel fun, they led him to Golgotha (which means "the place of the skull"). Jesus was so weak from his flogging and beatings that Simon of Cyrene was forced to help him carry his cross.

Mark does not give us the gory and cruel details of the crucifixion. He simply states, "And they crucified him" (Mark 15:24).

Mark records the soldiers casting lots for his clothes and the written notice that read, "THE KING OF THE JEWS." Those passing by hurled insults at him, and the chief priests and teachers of the law mocked him. Two "rebels" were crucified with him.

The cry of dereliction

Mark records only one of Jesus's seven sayings on the cross, but it is arguably the most important one. After three hours of darkness from noon to 3:00 p.m. on Good Friday, Jesus loudly cries out those awful words, "My God, my God, why have you forsaken me?" It was at this very moment that Jesus took the sins of mankind on himself and bore the full force of God's wrath for those sins. It was at this very moment that Jesus was forsaken by the Father, not relationally (because the Trinity cannot be separated) but judicially. The pain of God's wrath and judgment was far worse than the physical suffering of the crucifixion. It was this awful spiritual suffering that Jesus wanted to avoid in his prayer in the Garden of Gethsemane.

This is the very moment that "Jesus died for our sins." Or to use the apostle Paul's words, it was at this very moment that "he (God the Father) made him (Jesus the Messiah) who knew no sin to be sin on our behalf, so that we might become the righteousness of God in him (Jesus)" (2 Corinthians 5:21). This is the great doctrine of substitution.

Barabbas

My friend John Wayland, who I mentioned earlier, eloquently makes this profound comparison (which I have very slightly modified):

> Three crosses had already been built for that day's executions. Three criminals were sitting on "death row," and their crosses had already been prepared. All three of them deserved to die, and it was only a matter of time before the nails would pierce their hands or wrists. One of the criminals sitting on death row was Barabbas. He was an insurrectionist and convicted murderer. His crime carried with it the punishment of death. Death by crucifixion. Barabbas deserved to die. But it was Jesus who ended up being nailed to the cross prepared for Barabbas.

We are Barabbas

Then he makes this point: "You and I are Barabbas. You and I have sinned against God. The Scriptures make this clear: "For all have sinned and fall short of the glory of God" (Romans 3:23). And we know that the death penalty applies to us as we read, "the wages of sin is death" (Romans 6:23). We are Barabbas.

Set free

He then creates this personal and powerful application:

> Picture in your mind a cross with your name pinned to it leaning against the wall.

Realize that your rebellious attitude and actions have offended the Holy God of the universe, and your offense carries with it the sentence of death. Your cross had been built and you are sitting on death row. Imagine also, that as you sit in your cell, you hear your name being chanted, faintly at first, then stronger as time goes on. Others in the cell block realize that it is your name they are chanting and confirm that you are not just hearing things. Imagine the door at the end of the hall opening and guards walking straight to your cell with key in hand. They use the key to open wide your cell door. They step aside and say, "You are free to go! You are being released. Someone else will be using your cross today."

Takeaway

We deserved to die (physically, spiritually, and eternally) for our many sins. But Jesus the innocent and perfect Man died in our place. When we believe that, we are set free. Our sins are forgiven, and we are declared to be forever righteous (innocent of the sins we have committed) and given the gift of eternal life. Substitution is the heart of the gospel. It is the great demonstration of God's grace.

Have you believed this good news? Have you been "set free"? Perhaps God is tugging at your heart to make that commitment today.

THE RESURRECTION OF JESUS

Mark 15:40–16:8

> "Don't be alarmed," he (the angel) said. "You are looking for Jesus the Nazarene, who was crucified. He has risen. He is not here. See the place where they laid him. But go, tell his disciples and Peter, He is going ahead of you into Galilee. There you will see him, just as he told you." (Mark 16: 6–7)

Overview (Mark 15:40–16:8)

Jesus died at about 3:00 p.m. on Good Friday. Some of his female disciples witnessed his death. The women also saw Joseph of Arimathea take down the body of Jesus, wrap it in some linen clothes, and place Jesus in the tomb. They watched him roll the large stone against the entrance of the tomb at about 6:00 p.m. Then the women went to where they were staying to observe the Sabbath.

Early on Sunday morning, the women, Mary Magdalene, Mary the mother of James (perhaps Jesus's mother), and Salome go to the tomb to anoint Jesus's body. But when they arrived at the tomb, the stone had been rolled away, and an angel was sitting in the tomb. The angel announced those powerful epoch-changing words, "He is risen. He is not here."

The meaning of the resurrection

The resurrection of Jesus powerfully authenticated that he was indeed the Messiah, the Son of God. While his miracles, teaching, and presence demonstrated that he was the Son of God, the resurrection screamed out—He is the Messiah. He is who he claimed to be. The apostle Paul captures this crucial point with these words: "If Christ has not been raised, our preaching is useless and so is your faith." But then makes the nonnegotiable declaration on which Christianity is based, "But Christ has indeed been raised from the dead!" The resurrection of Jesus authenticates Christianity. It convinced the disciples that Jesus was the Messiah. The eleven fearful disciples became courageous proclaimers of the truth of the resurrection once they saw the resurrected Jesus.

The resurrection of Jesus is also proof that God accepted Jesus's death on the cross as payment in full for the sins of mankind. For our sins. We can know that our sins are forgiven because Jesus our Savior was raised from the dead. Mark repeatedly emphasizes that Jesus died and was buried so as to make the resurrection so clearly supernatural and climactic. The resurrection is the high point of Christ's first coming and the high point of our faith.

Mark's perspective

As many of you know, it is now accepted that Mark's gospel ends (rather abruptly) in chapter 16 verse 8. Verses 9–20 are not in the earliest manuscripts. So why does Mark end his Gospel with the women fleeing the tomb in fear and not going immediately to the disciples as the angel had instructed?

The disciples' failures

After Jesus's arrest in the Garden of Gethsemane, the male disciples ran away in fear. Peter, who followed at a distance, infamously denied Jesus three times. Mark's point is that the male disciples had failed to be faithful to Jesus. Except for Peter's denial, they do not appear after Jesus's arrest. They are AWOL! Only a few female disciples are present at his Crucifixion and burial—although at a distance. They showed more faithfulness and perseverance than the men.

On that resurrection Sunday morning, it was the women who came to the tomb. It seems that Mark highlights the absence of the male disciples when he has the women asking each other, "Who will roll the stone away?" There were no male disciples to help roll away the stone! They had bailed. They had failed their Master.

However, even the women, who proved significantly more faithful than the male disciples, failed to obey the angel's instruction to go tell the disciples that Jesus had risen. Instead, Mark has them running away in fear and saying "nothing to anyone." From the other Gospels, we know that they did eventually go and tell the disciples.

But Mark's point is that the male disciples had pretty much completely failed Jesus, and that even the female disciples, who proved to be more faithful, had also failed Jesus in the end.

Go back Galilee

So what's the thrust of this last chapter?

His disciples and Peter (who had most obviously failed Jesus) are instructed to go to Galilee and meet up with the resurrected Jesus. Go back to where you started your journey of discipleship with Jesus. The resurrected Jesus would forgive them for their faithlessness. He would give them a second chance. In his grace, he was offering them the opportunity to recommit to him and resume their journey of discipleship. It is interesting that the disciples did not immediately go to Galilee. It took the appearance of Jesus to the disciples in Jerusalem to motivate them to finally obey, go to Galilee, and accept Jesus's forgiveness and gracious offer of a second chance.

Do we need to go back to Galilee?

Perhaps for some of us, this has been a year of failure to follow Christ. Perhaps we are backsliding. Perhaps we've lost the joy of following Christ. Perhaps we feel like we are sometimes just going through the motions.

God's word to us today is—GO BACK TO GALILEE. The resurrected Jesus is there. He will forgive your sins and failures. Recommit to him and to your journey of discipleship. Make this your new year's resolution.

ABOUT THE AUTHOR

G. Brian Christie (ThM, Dallas Theological Seminary; JD, University of Texas), a transactional ("deal") law-yer, business executive, and company director, has taught men's Bible studies in churches in Texas, California, and Virginia over the past forty-five years. He has authored *12 Marks of a Man of God.*